The Bitton & Lugassy Edition

The MIRACLE WORKER

וזאת מצבת קבורה
הח"ח וזכר צדק קודש
התמלו"א ננ"ת המקובל האלק'
מורינו ורבינו רבי ראשונו
מימיו ומרנז בנן רמשפח ם
בנודר דר הסעולאדני
עמרם ן ריוואן
שנתבלקש יום ט' אבר ל" הקמבמכסיי
ש"ר ודאואן וקטשה נ"ם
עתמעעורתה הסול"ה נ"ות זכתו תעמוד לנו
ח נ צ ב ה

Stories about the Tzaddik
Rabbi Amram Ben Diwan

RABBI MEIR ELAZAR ATTIA

**SEPHARDIC
LEGACY SERIES**
PRESERVING SEPHARDIC HERITAGE
www.sephardiclegacy.com

To send stories, historic facts, letters, pictures, manuscripts and other
helpful material on the life of Rabbi Amram Ben Diwan *zt"l*, please
email the author at yazoulay@sephardiclegacy.com. This information
is necessary for future updated and revised editions of *The Miracle
Worker: Stories about the Tzaddik Rabbi Amram Ben Diwan*. He
who does so will be blessed in the merit of the Jewish nation.

Book & cover design by:

VIVIDESIGN
SRULY PERL | 845.694.7186
mechelp@gmail.com

Published and distributed by:

Israel Bookshop Publications
501 Prospect Street
Lakewood, NJ 08701
Tel: (732) 901-3009
Fax: (732) 901-4012
www.israelbookshoppublications.com
info@israelbookshoppublications.com

Printed in the USA

Distributed in Israel by:
Tfutza Publications
P.O.B. 50036
Beitar Illit 90500
972-2-650-9400

Distributed in Europe by:
Lehmanns
Unit E Viking Industrial Park
Rolling Mill Road,
Jarrow, Tyne & Wear NE32 3DP
44-191-406-0842

Distributed in Australia by:
Gold's Book and Gift Company
3-13 William Street
Balaclava 3183
613-9527-8775

Distributed in South Africa by:
Kollel Bookshop
Ivy Common
107 William Road, Norwood
Johannesburg 2192
27-11-728-1822

Tribute to Yehuda Azoulay

A special thank you to our dear friend, Yehuda Azoulay, who has devoted himself entirely to publishing this book, *The Miracle Worker: Stories about Rabbi Amram Ben Diwan.* He managed the entire project of the book from translation, financing, publishing, printing and distribution. Yehuda personally financed the entire project from the beginning as he felt this was his calling, and only later received financing for this project from generous sponsors. This quality testifies to what type of person Yehuda Azoulay is and his dedication toward the publication. Furthermore, we are very happy to have a collaboration with the Sephardic Legacy Series – Institute for Preserving Sephardic Heritage.

May the merit of this publication on the life of Rabbi Amram Ben Diwan bless him and his family, amen.

Sincerely,

Rabbi Meir Elazar Attia

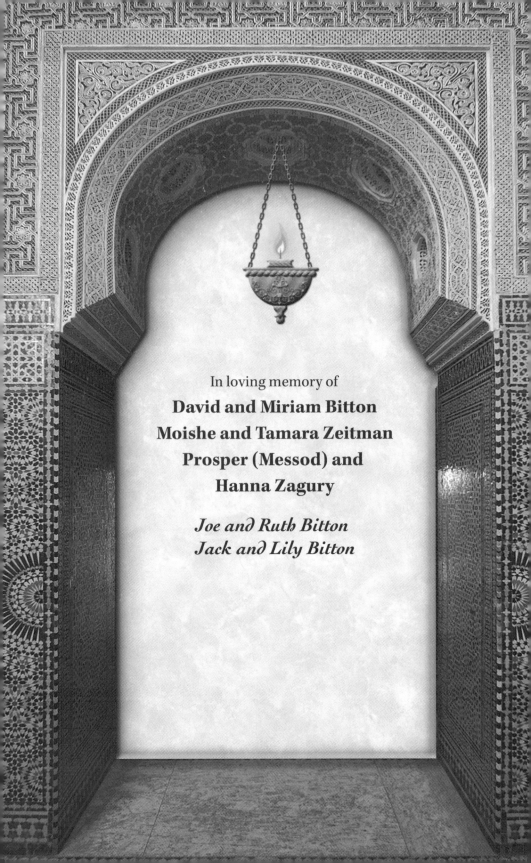

In loving memory of

David and Miriam Bitton

Moishe and Tamara Zeitman

Prosper (Messod) and

Hanna Zagury

Joe and Ruth Bitton

Jack and Lily Bitton

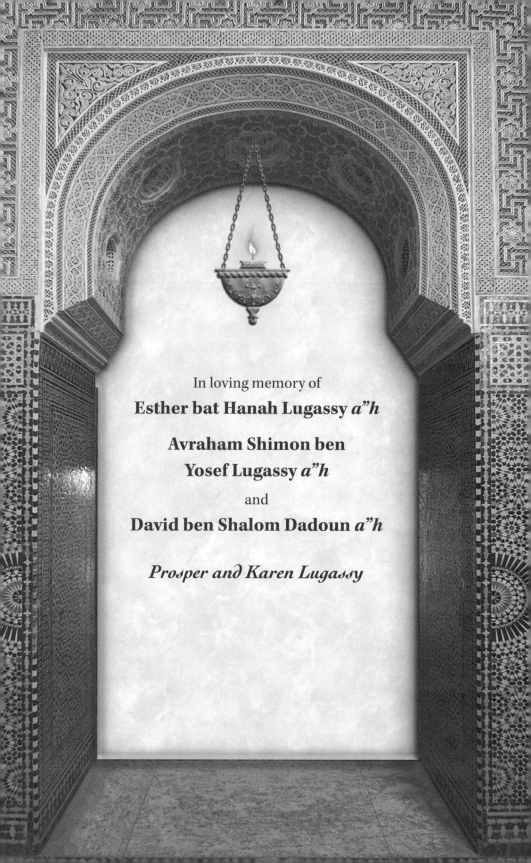

In loving memory of
Esther bat Hanah Lugassy *a"h*

**Avraham Shimon ben
Yosef Lugassy** *a"h*
and
David ben Shalom Dadoun *a"h*

Prosper and Karen Lugassy

Gold
Sponsors

Joe and Jack Bitton

Daniel and Brianna Bayer

Prosper and Karen Lugassy

Isaac and Fanny Queroub

Meyer Keslassy

Eric and Arona Benchetrit

Dr. Albert and Sherlin-Shira Baravarian

Gold
Sponsors

Joe and Esther Azoulay

Yehuda and Rena
Azoulay

Jacques and Vivian
Sayegh

Joe Dwek

Kenneth Applebaum

Yehuda Klein

Claude Bitton a"h

Table of Contents

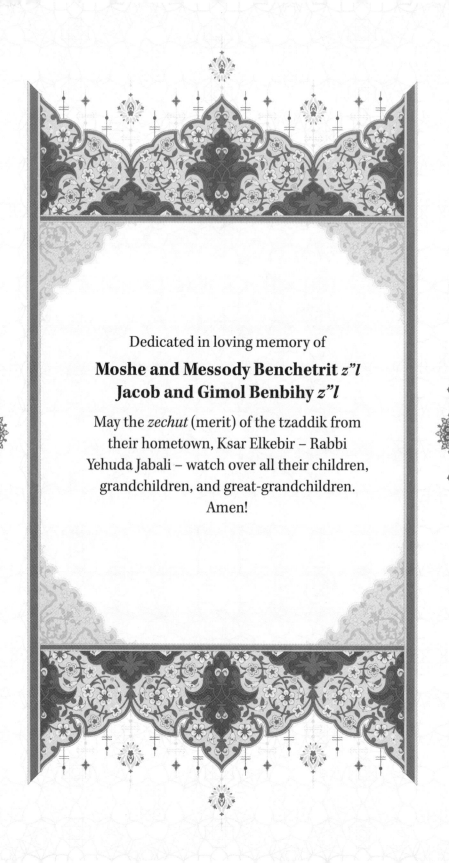

Dedicated in loving memory of

Moshe and Messody Benchetrit *z"l*
Jacob and Gimol Benbihy *z"l*

May the *zechut* (merit) of the tzaddik from
their hometown, Ksar Elkebir – Rabbi
Yehuda Jabali – watch over all their children,
grandchildren, and great-grandchildren.
Amen!

Acknowledgments

הודו לה׳ כי טוב כי לעולם חסדו

*Give thanks to Hashem, for He is good; His
kindness endures forever (Tehillim 136:1).*

FIRST AND FOREMOST, I OFFER MY HEARTFELT GRATITUDE TO
Hakadosh Baruch Hu, Who has guided me along the path of
truth and the righteous path of Torah. My heart overflows with
appreciation to Hashem for giving me the privilege of writing this
series of books, starting with the first volume of *A Legacy of Leaders*
until the ninth publication of Sephardic Legacy Series: *The Miracle
Worker: Stories about the Tzaddik Rabbi Amram Ben Diwan*, authored
by Rabbi Meir Elazar Attia.

I am indebted to Rabbi Joshua Bittan from Em Habanim
Sephardic Congregation, North Hollywood, California. He
mentioned several years ago to his cousin in Paris, France, Mr. Joel
Bittan, to contact me regarding the translation and formulation
of this publication about Rabbi Amram Ben Diwan. This book
would not have come to fruition without the assistance of Mr.
Joel Bittan. His enthusiasm, passion and dedication toward this
publication has been tremendous, and I am greatly thankful for all
his dedication toward this book.

I wish to extend my sincere gratitude to Mrs. Nehama Kohn, who translated material for this book. Thank you so much for all your devoted and outstanding work.

My sincerest thanks go to the editor of this volume, Chaya Silverstone, who painstakingly reviewed every minor detail in every chapter, page, and paragraph of the book, and also assisted with research and source material. Thank you, Miriam Allman, for your dedication in proofreading this entire book.

I am grateful as well to Mr. Sruly Perl for the magnificent interior and exterior design of this volume. Your unique touch and effects have profoundly enhanced this project, and I am very grateful to you for devoting so much of your time and talents to this book.

I would like to thank Israel Bookshop Publications, who are wonderful publishers and distributors and always a sheer delight to work with. Thank you R' Moshe Kaufman, Mrs. Liron Delmar, and your fantastic team for doing such a magnificent job at every single step of the way, and for making this undertaking as pleasant and efficient as possible.

Furthermore, I also wish to thank and bless the main sponsors of this publication, Joe and Jack Bitton, for their staunch support of the Sephardic Legacy Series. May G-d reward both the Bitton and Lugassy families abundantly for their kindness, and in the merit of Rabbi Amram Ben Diwan, may the Tzaddik bring you and your families much health, happiness and success in all your endeavors. It is through your generosity and assistance that this book has come to fruition.

It is with these words in mind that I humbly express my feelings of gratitude, affection, and admiration for the wonderful people who help and support the Sephardic Legacy Series – Institute for Preserving Sephardic Heritage. Through their selfless generosity, and with the Almighty's boundless grace and kindness, the institute has published thousands of books in English, French, and Hebrew. It is only with the loving support and assistance of each and every one of you that the institute has been able to achieve this remarkable level of success in preserving and perpetuating the glorious heritage of Sephardic Jewry. May Hashem bless each of you with much joy, success, and the ongoing ability and desire to make great contributions to Am Yisrael, amen.

Finally, I must thank my wife, Rena, who is my partner in everything that I do and everything that I am. I thank her especially for allowing me to spend countless hours on this holy work. May He bless us both with much *nahat* from our children, Esther Mazal, Yael, and Ovadia Yosef.

This book is the product of a translated book first published in Hebrew, then in French, and now accessible in the English language. Capturing the life of any remarkable figure is a challenge, and the difficulty is magnified when dealing with a personality from a country such as Morocco, which produced very little recorded documentation of its history and historical figures at the time. Despite my efforts to unearth information about this illustrious sage, I acknowledge the likelihood that there is important information about Rabbi Amram Ben Diwan that was missed, or that is simply inaccessible. Nevertheless, I hope and pray that I have succeeded in my mission to present an accurate portrait of one of the greatest Torah figures of the modern era.

It is my sincere prayer to Hashem that this book, *The Miracle Worker: Stories about the Tzaddik Rabbi Amram Ben Diwan*, authored by Rabbi Meir Elazar Attia, will serve as a great source of inspiration for Klal Yisrael, and motivate us all to draw closer to our Father in Heaven.

Yehuda Azoulay

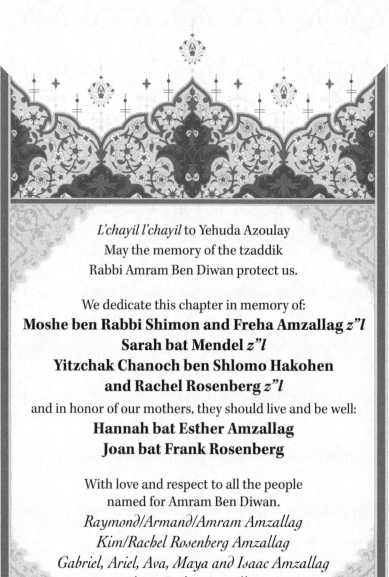

L'chayil l'chayil to Yehuda Azoulay
May the memory of the tzaddik
Rabbi Amram Ben Diwan protect us.

We dedicate this chapter in memory of:
Moshe ben Rabbi Shimon and Freha Amzallag *z"l*
Sarah bat Mendel *z"l*
Yitzchak Chanoch ben Shlomo Hakohen
and Rachel Rosenberg *z"l*
and in honor of our mothers, they should live and be well:
Hannah bat Esther Amzallag
Joan bat Frank Rosenberg

With love and respect to all the people
named for Amram Ben Diwan.
Raymond/Armand/Amram Amzallag
Kim/Rachel Rosenberg Amzallag
Gabriel, Ariel, Ava, Maya and Isaac Amzallag
Ilana Esther Amzallag
Eliahu David Amzallag

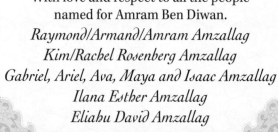

Introduction

Rabbi Amram, son of Rabbi Ephraim Diwan, was born in Jerusalem around the year 1740. His father's ancestors were natives of Diwan, an Arab village located south of Tangiers, Morocco. Every Jew born in this village was named Ben Diwan, "from Diwan."

After learning the revealed Torah from the Jerusalem scholars, Rabbi Amram went to a yeshiva of *mekubalim* in Hevron, where he began studying the esoteric part of the Torah.[1] He became one of the greatest sages of the Neve Shalom yeshiva founded by his uncle Rabbi Yehuda Diwan. He later settled in Hevron, where he learned Kabbalah.

In 1763, the yeshiva in Hevron encountered financial hardships, so its *hachamim* decided to send the tzaddik Rabbi Amram to Morocco to collect funds for the school. The Moroccan Jews

---

1. Among the sages learning with Rabbi Amram in the yeshiva were Rabbi Moshe Burla, *rosh yeshiva*; Rabbi Yisrael Yaakov Burla, later rabbi of Jerusalem; Rabbi Ephraim Navon, author of *Mahane Ephraim*; Rabbi Nissim Berachah, son-in-law of the Hida; Rabbi Eliyahu Parchi; Rabbi David Faraj; Rabbi Avraham ben Shushan; and Rabbi David Ashkenazi. In the morning, they studied halachah and in the afternoon, five pages of the *Reshit Hachmah* and the *Bet Yosef*.

had an intense love for the land of Israel; they would receive the representatives of the yeshivot with great honor and donate their last funds to supporting Torah study in the Holy Land.

In the following, written in 1763, the *hachamim* of the Hevron yeshiva introduce Rabbi Amram as their representative.

> For all these reasons, we have asked the great sage, learned and brilliant, our master Rabbi Amram Diwan, to represent us in his community…to make our difficult situation known to the public, with the hope that our financial situation will improve and that our city will not be emptied of its inhabitants, with G-d's help.
>
> Signed by the *hachamim* of Hevron
> *Aharon Alfandari*
> *Haim Yehuda Gomes Fato*
> *Yitzhak Zeevi*
> *Haim Rahamim Bajayo*
> *Eliyahu ben Archah*
> *Pinhas Mordechai Bajayo*
> *Avraham Gedalyah*[2]

The *hachamim* chose Rabbi Amram for this task for several reasons. The Tzaddik was a descendant of a member of the Moroccan community. For the rich donors of North Africa, it was a pleasure and great honor to see the child of a community member becoming a Torah scholar in the Holy Land, and they organized an appeal to assist him.

Another reason the Tzaddik was sent to Morocco was that during his life, Rabbi Amram was famous as a miracle worker whose

---

2. This letter is quoted in the book *Hakehillah Vehashadarim* by Rabbi David Ovadia, who mentions an exchange of letters between Rabbi Amram and the sages of Sefrou.

prayers were heard in Heaven. Everywhere he went, all of the Jews would run to receive his blessing for their *yeshuah* (deliverance).

Rabbi Amram was a *dayan* and a *gaon* in Torah. Whenever a rabbinical representative arrived in Morocco, the *hachamim* invited him to their yeshiva and presented their halachic queries and their difficulties in the Talmud. If he could answer their questions, the *hachamim* would accompany him and help him collect money during his stay. Wealthy Jews would even invite the scholar to their homes and their *smachot* along with the *hachamim* and notable community members.

The Moroccan *hachamim* were quick to recognize Rabbi Amram's greatness and his vast knowledge in halachah. In 1765, when the Tzaddik was staying in Fez, they asked him to examine their *psak* (ruling) and to approve it.[3] He replied, "Heaven approves that one should evaluate this synagogue only as it is now. I agree for all the above-mentioned reasons. I add my name simply to add a signature: the young Amram Diwan[4] sent by the holy *hachamim* from Eretz Yisrael." Rabbi Amram stayed in Morocco for about three years.

In 1773, the sages of Hevron asked him to go on a new mission for nine years—mainly so he could flee the town and escape the authorities, for he had disobeyed the order barring Jews from entering Me'arat Hamachpelah, the monument in which our saintly ancestors are buried, when he went there to pray for his son's health.[5]

---

3. This *psak* is quoted in *Mei Hashiloah* (62b) by Rabbi Refael Aharon Monsonego of Fez.

4. He signs "Amram Diwan" and not "Amram Ben Diwan." Jews from Morocco add the word *Ben* (*Ibn*) to their family names, for example: Ibn Denan, Ibn Ezra, Ibn Tzur, etc. Or, as we said earlier, he was called Ben Diwan, which means: from Diwan, because his forebears came from the town of Diwan. However, in his decisions, the Rabbi signed Amram Diwan only, or his initials: עד״י (Eden).

5. Rabbi Refael Baruch Toledano writes that according to community members of

During this final mission, while Rabbi Amram was visiting the pious singer of Meknes, Rabbi David Hashin, Rabbi Hashin wrote a poem in the Tzaddik's honor, to encourage the public to give generously for the yeshiva in Hevron:

> I shall sing a song of thanks before my Creator,
> In honor of the sage who delights me, my dear friend, this perfect man.
> My friends, my companions, listen to his words,
> Crown him with golden coins; I shall adorn him with crowns.[6]

When he arrived in Meknes in Tamuz of that year, the Tzaddik stayed at the home of Rabbi Zichri Messas, who welcomed all the *shadarim* (messengers) from Eretz Yisrael. Rabbi Messas established in his house a yeshiva where the *hachamim* of the city came to learn daily with Rabbi Amram. For eight years, Rabbi Mordechai Zichri, Rabbi David Hashin, and Rabbi Mordechai Sebban learned with him regularly.

On Shabbat *Parashat Shelah Lecha*,[7] Rabbi Amram, resembling an angel, delivered a discourse in the great synagogue of Rabbi Refael Berdugo. In his long, impassioned sermon, he encouraged his listeners to settle in the Holy Land. Impressed by his words, the community expressed its desire to move to Eretz Yisrael. The mayor then summoned the Tzaddik, as well as the *hachamim* and the community's president, Mr. Shelomo Mimran, to declare that

---

Ouazzane, Rabbi Amram arrived in Meknes in Adar 1775 and stayed there until Rosh Hodesh Elul of 1782, when he left for Fez. He stayed there until the month of Tamuz and made the trip with a caravan to the village of Asjen, where he passed away on the night of Tisha BeAv, on Shabbat. It was not until the following Thursday that the news arrived in Meknes, where the *rabbanim* eulogized him.

6. This song appears in Rabbi Hashin's book, *Tehilah LeDavid*, p. 47.

7. Taken from the introduction to *Otzar Hamichtavim*, part 1, p. 12, by Rabbi Yosef Messas, grandson of Rabbi Zichri.

the Jews were forbidden to leave, as the entire town depended on their crafts and trades.

Because of minor warfare taking place at the time,[8] Rabbi Amram was only able to leave Meknes after seven years. He departed with his host Rabbi Messas, who decided to accompany him to Eretz Yisrael. Together they traveled to Fez, where they stayed for one or two years. In Fez, Rabbi Zichri took sick and passed away on Erev Rosh Hashanah 5542/1782.[9] His friend Rabbi Amram pronounced a heartfelt eulogy, in which he extolled the deceased's wisdom and piety.

Rabbi Amram continued his journey alone to Sefrou, from where, together with a caravan, he visited all the villages where Jews lived, up to the village of Asjen. He caught pneumonia and was ill. He felt that his hour had come. He summoned the members of the *Hevra Kadisha* and asked them to bury him in the Jewish cemetery in Asjen, under the olive tree near the entrance. He did not want a *matzevah* (monument) erected; he asked for no more than a simple stone on his grave. Some say that, following his burial, Rabbi Amram appeared in a dream to the head of the *Hevra Kadisha* to make this request.

According to some opinions, the Tzaddik left this world on Tisha BeAv 5542/1782. The day of his *hillula* is the seventh day after his death, 15 Av, a date established as a day of rejoicing for the Jewish people, as the Talmud states.[10]

His demise constituted a great loss for the Jewish people. The

---

8. Introduction to the book *Mayim Haim*, p. 19. Nevertheless, in *Otzar Hamichtavim*, he writes that they stayed in Fez only a few days, which means he remained in Meknes for eight years.

9. This is according to the opinion that Rabbi Amram Ben Diwan did not pass away on 9 Av 1782, but rather on a later date.

10. *Ta'anit* 26b and 31a.

Tzaddik was eulogized publicly in all the cities and towns of Morocco. People related how many sick people had been cured and how much suffering was averted because of him. "I shed tears because of the terrible news! The Holy Land has lost a great man," cried Rabbi David Hashin.

The *hachamim* revealed a sign of the Tzaddik's death based on the verse *Badu bane ad mashber*—"The sons came up to the delivery seat."[11] The letters עד (*ad*) are the initials of the name *Amram Diwan*, and the word משבר (*mashber*) has the same numerical value (542) of the year of his death, תקמ"ב.

May his merit protect us.

---

11. *Yeshayahu* 37:3.

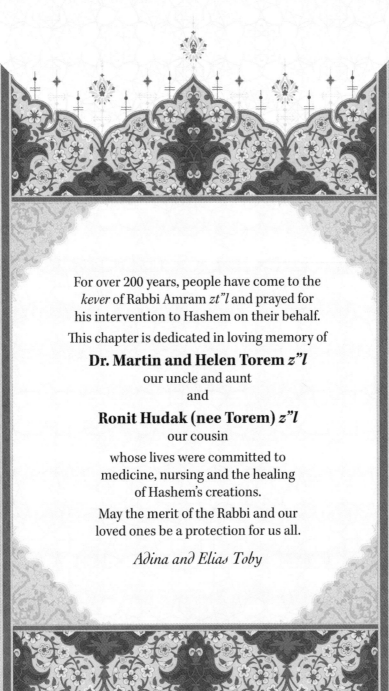

For over 200 years, people have come to the *kever* of Rabbi Amram *zt"l* and prayed for his intervention to Hashem on their behalf.

This chapter is dedicated in loving memory of

Dr. Martin and Helen Torem *z"l*
our uncle and aunt
and

Ronit Hudak (nee Torem) *z"l*
our cousin

whose lives were committed to medicine, nursing and the healing of Hashem's creations.

May the merit of the Rabbi and our loved ones be a protection for us all.

Adina and Elias Toby

Dedicated in memory of
David Revivo *z"l*

by Victor and Ilana Arrobas
David and Elana Bitton

Brief History of
Moroccan Jewry

JEWISH COMMUNITIES HAVE EXISTED IN MOROCCO SINCE AS EARLY as 70 CE. It was during the end of the Second Temple era when the first group of Jews moved to North Africa, and a second large wave of migration from the Iberian Peninsula occurred in the period leading up to and following the Spanish Inquisition in 1492.

687 | The Beginning of Jewish Morocco

Approximately thirty thousand Jews fled after the destruction of the Second Temple to the Maghreb area (Morocco, Algeria and Tunisia), which was at the time inhabited by Berber tribes.

800 | Fez—City of Scholars

During the early ninth century, the great yeshivot of Babylon passed the torch to several heirs, among them the Jewish center in the city of Fez, in northeastern Morocco. The golden age of the Jewish community in Fez lasted for nearly three hundred years. Fez was known to be the city of scholars, and their contribution toward Torah works and growth as a vibrant spiritual center was influenced throughout all of Morocco.

From the ninth to eleventh centuries, its yeshivot (religious schools) attracted brilliant scholars, poets and grammarians. Sages such as Dunash Ibn Labrat and Rabbi Yitzhak Alfasi spent most of their lives in Fez before they migrated to Spain. The invasions of the Almohades, fanatic Muslim sects, caused destruction and suffering to the Jewish community in Fez, just as it did throughout Andalusia. The most famous refugee from the Almohade terror in Fez was Rabbi Moses ben Maimon (Maimonides), who escaped with his family to Egypt in 1165. He had lived in Fez for five years after being uprooted from his home in Cordoba, Spain.

1146 | Almohad Dynasty (1146 through fifteenth century)

The Almohad Caliphate was a Moroccan Berber Muslim movement founded in the twelfth century. In order not to fall prey to the cruelty of the Almohad dynasty, which seized control of Morocco in 1146, the Jews were forced to choose between two options: die or convert. Some chose a third option: to become *animi* (crypto-Jews), which is to say, Jews at home and Muslims in public. This situation roused Maimonides, who lived in Fez at the time, to write his famous "Epistle on Martyrdom," which gave the *animi* permission to live in an uncertain state of identity, until the need should pass.

1492 | Spanish Inquisition

The Spanish Inquisition was a religious committee established in 1478 by Catholic Monarchs King Ferdinand II of Aragon and Queen Isabella I of Castile, Spain. The word Inquisition literally means "detailed or relentless questioning." Therefore, the Inquisition, or one would call it "Expulsion," worked in large part to guarantee the orthodoxy of converts.

The Inquisition was extremely enforced between the years of

1480 and 1530. One would think the Inquisition only took place in that year of 1492. Yet persecution and all sorts of brutal acts went on for fifty years. The Jewish expulsion had been the main project of the Spanish Inquisition, headed by Tomas de Torquemada. Torquemada believed that as long as the Jews remained in Spain, they would influence the tens of thousands of recent Jewish converts to Christianity to continue practicing Judaism. King Ferdinand and Queen Isabella rejected Torquemada's demand that the Jews be expelled until January 1492, when the Spanish Army defeated Muslim forces in Granada, thereby restoring the whole of Spain to Christian rule.

On March 30, they issued the expulsion decree, the order to take effect in precisely four months. The short time span was a great gain to the rest of Spain, as the Jews were forced to clear up their homes and businesses at ridiculously low prices. Throughout those disturbing times, Spanish priests actively encouraged Jews to convert to Christianity.

King Ferdinand changed his mind about the Jewish refugees and withstood this pressure when he realized that they might be an asset to his country and so should be kept in Portugal. Therefore, few ships were provided for the exodus, so few Jews left. Those remaining were accused of having violated the original agreement and, in accordance with its terms, were declared slaves and handed over to Christian masters, unless they accepted baptism.[1]

Like other cases in Jewish history when Jews were uprooted, in the Spanish expulsion too there was no great desire among most nations to take in the Jewish refugees. One exception was King Muhammad al-Sheikh, a ruler kind enough to open his country

---

1. *Community Magazine*, April 2009, "Rabbi Don Isaac Abarbanel and the Spanish Inquisition," by Yehuda Azoulay, pp. 42-44.

to the Jews fleeing Spain. The refugees from Spain settled mostly in the urban communities of Fez, Meknes, Sale and Marrakesh and other cities.

Spanish Jews moved to Morocco to escape persecution on the Iberian Peninsula. When the refugees from the Inquisition arrived in the country at the end of the fifteenth century, they found a substantial Jewish community already in place. Unfortunately, the native Moroccan Jewish community greeted the newcomers with a degree of hostility. The Jews of Morocco feared that the Spanish émigrés would bring commercial competition, and, more generally, they saw themselves as superior to the Jews of Spain. They went so far as to question the religious sincerity of the new arrivals—even though these Jews had just courageously opted to leave their home country to avoid forced conversion.

Despite the hostility, the Spanish Jews eventually dominated the communities in which they settled, and Fez became their cultural center. They established their own synagogues and communal institutions, and their rabbis instituted many *takanot* (enactments), known as the "*takanot* of the exile of Castile," which were based on Spanish Jewish tradition and dealt with matters such as marriage, divorce, and inheritance. The majority of the Spanish exiles in Morocco thus managed to maintain their Spanish identity in their new homeland and build a thriving community.[2]

1631 | Alawite Dynasty

The year 1631 brought the rise of the Alawite dynasty, which rules Morocco to this day. The rulers of this house treated the Jews warmly, allowing them to find their way to key positions in high places, as royal mint managers, royal treasurers and more.

---

2. *A Legend of Greatness: The Life and Times of Hacham Haim Yosef David Azoulay*, p. 44, by Yehuda Azoulay. Israel Bookshop Publications, February 2013.

1739 | The Printing Presses of Jewish Morocco

While the printing press was invented in Germany back in the fifteenth century, it had yet to be heard of in Morocco. Rabbi Haim Ben Attar was the author of *Or HaHaim* ("Light of Life"). It was fate that drove Ben Attar to make *aliyah* in 1739, after a bitter inheritance dispute within his family. En route to Israel, Rabbi Haim Ben Attar stopped in Livorno, Italy, where he printed his books, and assisted Moroccan rabbinical figures in printing their Torah works. The first printing presses in Morocco were from Jews and much of the influence was from Rabbi Haim Ben Attar's correspondence with its Moroccan Jewish leaders.

For many centuries, the Jews and Muslims in Morocco enjoyed, what was for the most part, a peaceful coexistence. The juxtaposition of the two cultures is believed to be largely responsible for the numerous similarities between Moroccan Jews and Muslims.

But while the Jewish communities were generally safe, there were also periods when the Moroccan kingdom vigorously enforced the laws pertaining to the second-class *dhimmi*[3] status of its Jewish citizens. Urban Jews were forced to live in ghettos called *mellahs*, a name derived from the Arabic word for salt. Muslims in these periods would force Jews to salt the heads of executed prisoners before their public display, and thus the urban Jewish quarters became known by this name. As it turned out, the Jews only benefited from this policy of segregation. Living apart enabled them to practice their religion more freely without the interference of troublesome neighbors. It also minimized, to a large extent, the level of anti-Semitism, as the saying goes, "out of sight, out of mind."

---

3. The Arabic word *dhimmi* literally means "protected citizen." The formal status of *dhimmi*, however, was for Jews in Muslim lands an official and legalized state of second-class citizenship. There was no official status of *dhimmi* for the Jews in Morocco.

The Moroccan monarchy established a unique relationship with this essential *dhimmi* minority, one which remained in place even until recent times.

1900 | The Modern Era

The nineteenth century, which brought emancipation to the Jews of many countries, failed to fundamentally alter the status of Moroccan Jews, but produced new divisions among them and entailed new sources of trouble. The war with France in 1844 brought new misery and ill treatment upon the Moroccan Jews, especially upon those of Mogador (known as Essaouira). When the war with Spain broke out on September 22, 1859, the Moors had nothing more fitting to do than to plunder the houses of friendly Jewish families in Tetuan. Most of the Jews saved their lives only by fleeing. About four hundred were killed. A like result followed the conflict with Spain in 1853 in consequence of the violent acts of the cliff-dwellers in Melilla. During this century and up to 1910, around one thousand Moroccan Jewish families migrated to Amazon, in northern Brazil, during the rubber boom.

In 1912 the signing of the Treaty of Fez turned Morocco into a French colony. For the Jews of Morocco this treaty signaled the end of a dark period replete with pogroms, and the beginning of a new era in which the Jews enjoyed a cultural, social, and political renaissance. During these years the teaching of Hebrew, combined with the ideas of Enlightenment (both the general kind and Jewish Haskala), spread throughout Morocco via the global Jewish school network Alliance Israelite Universelle (translated into Hebrew as "All Israel Are Friends"), which took the children of Morocco under its wings. It was then that the Jews of Morocco began to exit the *mellahs* (the Jewish quarters, somewhat akin to the European ghettos) and move to the new European-style neighborhoods in the major cities.

1940 | King Muhammad V and the Holocaust

In 1940 the Nazis conquered France and established the Vichy regime. During World War II, King Muhammad V refused to implement the anti-Semitic laws imposed upon his province by the Nazi-controlled Vichy regime in France that ruled parts of Morocco at that time. Many historians are divided as to the extent to which Moroccan King Muhammad V complied with the edicts of the Vichy regime. Regardless, the Jews were soon expelled from government positions and thrown back into the ghetto-like *mellah*. In 1942 the Allies conquered Morocco and stopped the plans of the Nazi death machine in North Africa.

1948 | The Establishment of the State of Israel and Moroccan Jewish *Aliyah*

The establishment of the State of Israel caused much excitement among the Jews of Morocco. Nevertheless, this was not just due to love of their people, but also resulted from the hardships of life in Morocco. Between 1948 and 1956 some 85,000 Jews made *aliyah* from Morocco. The immigrants were forced to adjust to the national "melting pot." Thousands of them were led in the dead of night to frontier settlements in order to man and populate the borders. Eventually these settlements would come to be known as "Development Towns" (*Ayarot Pituach*). This trauma stayed with the immigrants for many years, and found expression in Israeli music, literature and even film.

1956 | Morocco's Independence

In February of 1956, Morocco acquired limited rule. Further negotiations for full independence culminated in the French-Moroccan Agreement signed in Paris on March 2, 1956. On April 7, 1956, France officially relinquished its protectorate in Morocco.

In 1956 Morocco was liberated from French rule, and banned the Jews living in its territory from immigrating to Israel. One reason was apparently the important role played by the Jews in the Moroccan economy. In 1960 the Israeli Mossad embarked on a daring mission to smuggle the Jews of Morocco to Israel aboard the fishing vessel Egoz. On one of its excursions the ship sank near the Straits of Gibraltar, and nearly all those aboard perished, including forty-four immigrants. The disaster drew significant global notice, followed by international pressure on Morocco, until it relented, allowing its Jews to leave under various restrictions. Between 1961 and 1967 approximately 120,000 Jews made *aliyah* from Morocco to Israel.

In 2014 the Jewish community of Morocco numbered around 2,500 people, as opposed to 204,000 Jews who lived in the country in 1947. Many of the Jews of Morocco also immigrated to other countries, including France, Canada and the United States. Before the founding of Israel in 1948, there were approximately 250,000 to 350,000 Jews residing in Morocco, which gave Morocco the largest Jewish community in the Sephardic world, but fewer than 2,500 or so remain today.

Yehuda Azoulay, editor of *The Miracle Worker: Stories about the Tzaddik Rabbi Amram Ben Diwan*, at the *kever* of Rabbi Amram Ben Diwan. The event took place in May 2016 when Yehuda Azoulay led a delegation called "North American Conference of Moroccan Jewry—Continuing to further Judeo–Muslim Dialogue & Intercultural Relations."

A *sefer Torah* inauguration in loving memory of Rabbi Amram Ben Diwan in May 2015.

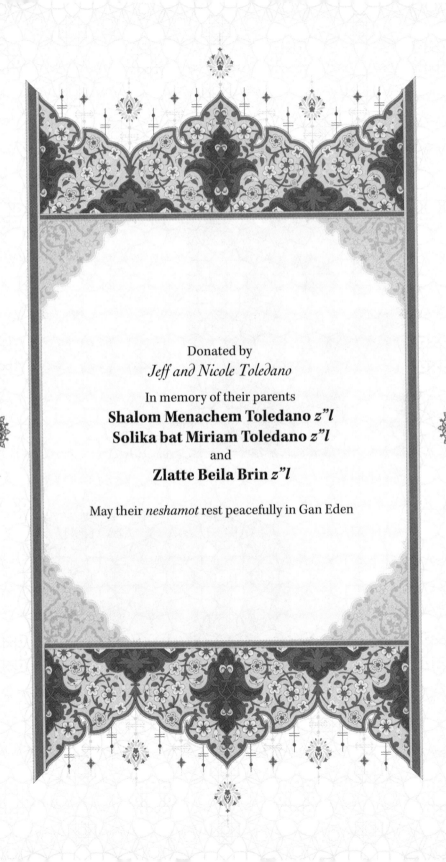

Donated by
Jeff and Nicole Toledano

In memory of their parents
Shalom Menachem Toledano *z"l*
Solika bat Miriam Toledano *z"l*
and
Zlatte Beila Brin *z"l*

May their *neshamot* rest peacefully in Gan Eden

CHAPTER ONE

Rabbi Amram Ben Diwan

An Act of Kindness

Rabbi Amram Ben Diwan's greatness was manifest not only in his holy behavior and intensive Torah study, but also in his dedication to helping his brethren.[1]

An impoverished but decent man in Fez was about to marry his son to an orphaned girl, but he did not have money to cover the wedding expenses. Too embarrassed to ask for assistance, he went to Rabbi Amram, who was then staying in Fez, and told him about his hardships. In a delicate financial situation himself, the Tzaddik did not have money to help the man. Out of pity, he gave him his Shabbat coat to auction among the wealthy men in town.

When the news became known, all the rich Jews who valued Torah offered high sums for the Tzaddik's coat. In the end, one of the men bought it for an amount that covered all the wedding

---

1. Rabbi Aharon Monsonego, chief rabbi of Morocco, told the following story when he visited Rabbi Amram's grave on the *hillula* on 15 Av 5756/July 31, 1996. Here is what his ancestors, living in Fez, told him.

The rabbis, the teachers, and the heads of the community of Ouazzane.
From left to right: Rabbi Shalom Israel, the director of Talmud Torah; Mr.
Eliyahu Elhadad, head of the community; Rabbi Eliyahu Malka, *hacham*
and *dayan* of the town; Rabbi Refael Abou, inspector of all the *talmude*
Torah of Morocco; and other teachers and students of the community.

expenses. Rabbi Amram came to the wedding, happy to have
performed this act of benevolence.

Figs from Gan Eden[2]

In Taza, Morocco, Rabbi Amram and his son Rabbi Haim were
invited to stay in the home of a man named Benchimol. Once,
when Rabbi Haim became gravely ill, his father prayed for him
and Rabbi Haim recovered. He later craved figs and asked his
father to bring him some; however, it was not fig season.

---

2. See *Malchei Rabbanan*, p. 102.

Rabbi Amram asked his host if he could purchase figs for his son.

"Rabbi," said the man, astonished. "Where can I buy you figs? There are none to be found!"

"At the market, and may G-d give you success."

Benchimol could not disobey the Tzaddik. He went to the market, expecting to come back empty-handed.

At the market, a non-Jew came to Benchimol and offered to sell him some figs.

"Idiot!" Benchimol answered. "Do you take me for a fool?" He couldn't believe this man honestly had figs to sell.

The Arab took five beautiful ripe figs out of his coat. Stunned by this miracle, Benchimol purchased the fruit and brought them to the Tzaddik.

Rabbi Amram explained to his host, "These figs came from Gan Eden especially for my son Rabbi Haim!"

A *Segulah* for Bearing Boys[3]

During the Tzaddik's stay in Fez, he stayed at the home of Rabbi Menashe ibn Denan. Rabbi Menashe and his wife were blessed with several daughters. However, they were distressed because they had not yet been blessed with a son.

During Rabbi Amram's stay, Mrs. Denan gave birth to another daughter. According to Moroccan custom, the father asks a rabbi to bless his newborn daughter at the name-giving ceremony. When they asked Rabbi Amram to bless their baby, he immediately gave the name Fadina, which means "finished," as if to say that her mother had ceased having girls. Indeed, later, this couple had only sons.

---

3. Yosef ben Naim, *Malchei Rabbanan*, "Amram Elbaz," p. 102b; Rabbi Yosef Messas, *Otzar Hamichtavim*, vol. I, introduction.

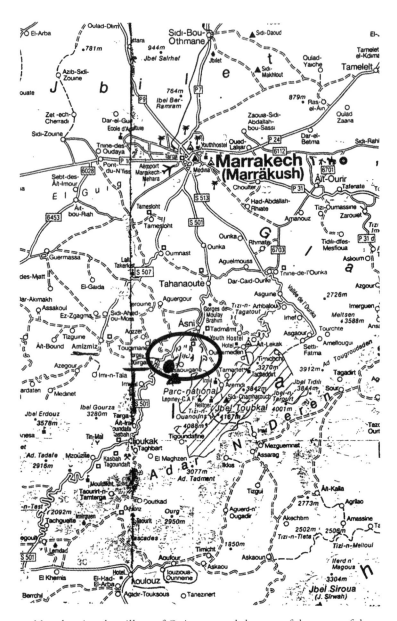

Map showing the village of Ouirgane, and the area of the grave of the
tzaddik Rabbi Haim Ben Diwan, at 90 km south of Marrakesh.

Me'arat Hamachpelah[4]

Following Rabbi Amram's return from his first mission in Morocco, his son's health worsened from day to day. The Tzaddik wanted to pray for his health at Me'arat Hamachpelah, the burial place of our ancestors Avraham, Yitzhak, and Yaakov.

At that time, Jews were only allowed to approach up to the seventh step of the entrance. Rabbi Amram requested full entry from the Arab guard there. The guard permitted the Tzaddik to disguise himself as an Arab and enter the burial place along with the respectable Muslims who would pray at the Me'arat Hamachpelah mosque on Friday afternoons. The guard warned Rabbi Amram that he would not help him if he was discovered.

As planned, father and son mixed in with the crowd of Arabs entering the building. They quickly went to pray near the graves of the *Avot*. Unfortunately, a man recognized the Rabbi and ran to tell the guard that he had seen two Jews praying. The guard immediately closed the doors to the building, to prevent a gathering inside. (Some write that this cruel guard had deliberately closed the doors to prevent Rabbi Amram and his son from fleeing, and had denounced them to the governor.)

He then leaped forward and called out, "Jews came into Me'arat Hamachpelah!" The excited crowd ran in hot pursuit of the two Jews. The news was immediately related to the town governor (the pasha), who declared that the lives of Rabbi Amram and his son were free for the taking; anyone who found them could kill them. By a miracle, an opening materialized in the building through which the Tzaddik and his son escaped.[5]

---

4. Mr. Moshe Dahan related this story, originally told by the tzaddik Rabbi Yosef Messas, whose great-grandfather had welcomed Rabbi Amram in his home for over eight years.

5. Dayan Rabbi Yaakov Toledano bar Moshe writes in one of his poems in honor of Rabbi

Thanks to their Arab attire, the pair did not alert the attention of passersby as they fled far from the site. That same Friday, they arrived at the docks in Jaffa and boarded a boat headed for Constantinople. From Turkey, they continued their journey to Morocco.

In Morocco, Rabbi Amram purchased a small one-room apartment in the Jewish quarter, in which they lived. When he journeyed to collect funds, he left his son alone in that room. Rabbi Haim's state of health would worry his father constantly. In a letter that Rabbi Amram wrote to his grandfather, the Tzaddik gave his grandfather permission, in case something happened to him, to sell that room and give the money to Rabbi Haim. (That letter still exists today.)

The Tzaddik Passes Away

Before leaving the town of Sefrou, Morocco, the Tzaddik was very worried by Rabbi Haim's poor health. Lifting his eyes to Heaven, he prayed, "Master of the universe! May I be his atonement! Give my son life and take me in his place! I have no more strength to tend to him. Please help us!"

His son's health suddenly improved, so Rabbi Amram decided to continue his journey to collect funds, joining a large caravan crossing the mountains. He arrived in Asjen, about six miles from Ouazzane, and fell ill. A few days after his arrival, Rabbi Amram returned his soul to his Maker on the ninth of Av 5542/1782.

The *Hevra Kadisha* of Asjen, a town numbering thirty families, arranged the Tzaddik's funeral. The news spread rapidly in

Amram, "G-d made a gracious miracle for them and they escaped their enemies." See *Yismah Yisrael*, liturgics according to the tradition of Meknes Jews.

Morocco and many Jews came to pray at his grave. Lamentations and poems were written in his honor.

Since the ninth of Av is a day of mourning for the Jewish people, they could not make his *hillula* that day; they put it off until the fifteenth of Av, seven days later. Since then, throngs visit his grave on the *hillula* date.

The Shelah explains that Yom Kippur is a day of atonement and the granting of prayers before our Creator. Similarly, the day of the death of a tzaddik is a day of Divine favor. Although it is a day of mourning, it is a day of *hillula*, of celebration, in the Heavenly Assembly.[6]

---

6. See *Hashushelet Leveth Pinto*, p. 37.

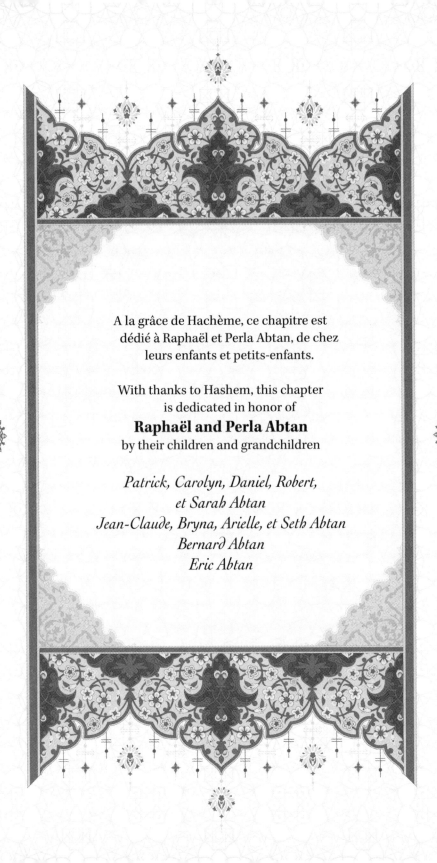

CHAPTER TWO

Rabbi Haim Ben Diwan

The Passing of Rabbi Haim[1]

FOLLOWING RABBI AMRAM'S DEATH IN 1782, HIS SON RABBI HAIM carried on his mission for the Hevron yeshiva. It is said that two years after his father's death, he purchased a courtyard in Asjen and sold it afterwards.[2] We also know that he came there to receive his father's inheritance.

Rabbi Haim traveled from village to village, from the north of Morocco to the south. After visiting the towns of Essaouira and Marrakesh, he arrived exhausted in Ouirgane, near Araz, south of Marrakesh, his clothes tattered and torn. He fell sick and his health worsened from day to day. While struggling with his illness, he spoke to Jews living in nearby villages about the greatness of Jerusalem and encouraged them to travel to the Holy Land. He

---

1. See a similar story in *Bemehitzat Hachamim VeRabbanim* by Rabbi Yaakov Lasry.

2. Rabbi Yaakov Toledano in *Megilat Starim*, cited in *Mizrah Uma'hacham*, p. 380. He attests that he saw the written documents dated 1744. It is plausible that Rabbi Haim died that same year.

Map showing the burial place of the tzaddikim of Morocco.

also taught the sages the secrets of the Torah, as his father had done in the major towns of Morocco.

After resting a little, Rabbi Haim was suddenly inspired and understood that he would soon be called back to the Heavenly Assembly. He prepared himself to die in purity and sanctity.

Near the place where he was standing, he heard the sound of a tumultuous watercourse, similar to a cascade. He went down to the stream and immersed there. He then covered his body with the shrouds he had taken with him and returned his soul to his Maker.

The people standing by related that the earth opened up and Rabbi Haim's body fell inside. Nearby was a well covered by a large stone, which was used by the shepherds to draw water for their sheep. When the shepherds lifted the stone, following Rabbi Haim's death, it flew from their hands and rolled to the pit where the Tzaddik's body was lying. It stopped there as if someone had set it at that precise place. This massive stone marks Rabbi Haim's grave to this day.

The shepherds who witnessed this episode never tried moving the stone. The Arab village where this well was found was called Araz. One night following his death, Rabbi Haim revealed himself to the village chief, Mubarak. "Wake up!" he said. "Go tell the Jews who live in Tachnat, Isni, and Amergan, to the south of Marrakesh, that on the hill, under the big stone, is buried a Jew named Rabbi Haim Ben Diwan. If you perform this mission faithfully, know that you and your descendants will know no lack your entire lifetime." The Arab woke up in shock and went to the Jews of these villages to relate his dream and the sage's request.

After collecting the necessary funds, the Jews brought building stones and tools and built a beautiful *matzevah* on Rabbi Haim's grave. Afterwards, they decided to build a synagogue nearby in which they put *sifre Torah*, exactly like the synagogue near his father's grave in Asjen. His grave subsequently became a site visited by many on the day of his *hillula*. Among the visitors, many Arab men and women came to pray to G-d to cure them. The Arabs guarded the site with utmost care and, now that most Jews have left Morocco, they continue to care for it.

The day of Rabbi Haim's passing and burial was established as his annual *hillula*, a sign that his soul rejoices with us. Many people come to his grave and request, "Show us wonders as your father Rabbi Amram did!"

No tree grew above Rabbi Haim's grave, though numerous pigeons would perch above the houses and even nested on their roofs. This pleased the pilgrims and encouraged them to pray and rejoice, feeling a sense of unity. The pilgrims did not light a large number of candles as they did on Rabbi Amram's grave in Asjen, and no stones surrounded Rabbi Haim's *matzevah*.

The committee in charge of the site purchased long white candles and then sold them at an auction; sold in the name of famous tzaddikim, they sold for a steep price. The auction money was used to keep the site in good order and to hire a guard.

Rumors circulated about the miracles performed in this place. All the natives called him "Rabbi Haim Esba (the Lion)" and the number of participants at the *hillula* grew every year. The admirers of Rabbi Haim Ben Diwan made his name known everywhere.

The Holy Son[3]

Rabbi Haim Ben Diwan promoted faith and fear of Heaven in Morocco. He helped the poor from every segment of the population. His influence on the community was so great that around his grave prayers are offered concerning every event of a

---

3. These stories were told by Rabbi Yosef Halevi, rabbi of Katzrin, Israel, whose family is from Ouirgane.

person's life—from finding a marriage partner to having children, offering thanks for a *brit milah* and bar mitzvah, and so on.

There is no doubt that the Tzaddik left an imprint on Morocco during his life; even after his death, many stories were related about him.[4]

An hour and a half ride south of Marrakesh is the village of Ouirgane. A stream flows in the middle of the village, flanked by a restaurant from where a dirt path leads to the grave of Rabbi Haim. The inhabitants show the road to those who wish to visit the holy site, a ten-minute walk from the restaurant. There they built hotel rooms, a synagogue, and a well-tended courtyard guarded by two older Arab men. A few steps away is the tomb, inside a small room. The hospitality displayed there is due to the influence of the tzaddik buried there.

The Tzaddik Protects

The tzaddik Rabbi Haim protects those who visit his grave. Once, an Arab guard tried stealing food from a family while they were asleep. Rabbi Haim came to the guard in a dream and ordered him to return what he had stolen and to ask forgiveness from the family. While they were still sleeping, the guard returned all the food and when they awoke, he told them about the dream and asked their forgiveness.

The residents of Ouirgane related that an Arab guard complained to the deceased Tzaddik that he did not have enough money for the approaching sacrificial festival. He was still speaking when he heard a ram bleating. He looked in the direction of the sound and saw a ram caught by his horns. The guard made a vow to sacrifice

---

4. When Rabbi Haim became gravely ill, his father made a special *tikun* and asked G-d for him to die instead of his son. Rabbi Haim then recovered and, some time later, Rabbi Amram passed away near Ouazzane.

the ram on the Tzaddik's grave and to keep guard in that place until his death.

First page of the book written by Rabbi Yehuda Ben Diwan, son of the
first Rabbi Amram, uncle of the tzaddik Rabbi Amram Ben Diwan.
He was one of the sages of Jerusalem and had signed the approval
of the book *Rishon Letzion* of Rabbi Haim Ben Attar.

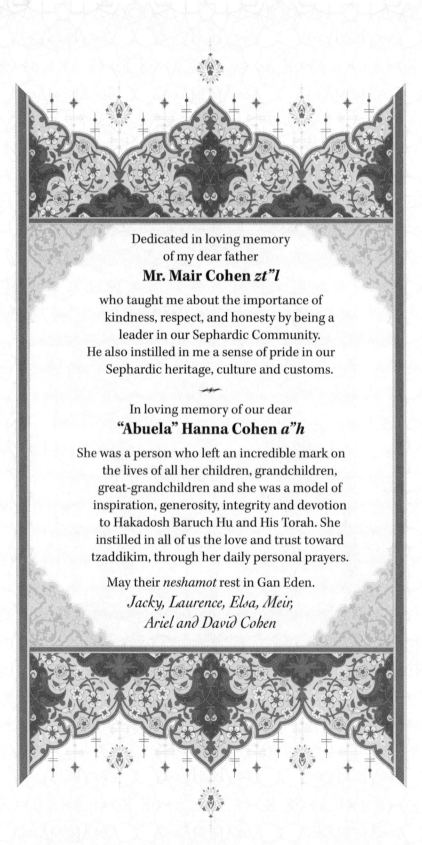

Dedicated in loving memory
of my dear father
Mr. Mair Cohen *zt"l*

who taught me about the importance of
kindness, respect, and honesty by being a
leader in our Sephardic Community.
He also instilled in me a sense of pride in our
Sephardic heritage, culture and customs.

In loving memory of our dear
"Abuela" Hanna Cohen *a"h*

She was a person who left an incredible mark on
the lives of all her children, grandchildren,
great-grandchildren and she was a model of
inspiration, generosity, integrity and devotion
to Hakadosh Baruch Hu and His Torah. She
instilled in all of us the love and trust toward
tzaddikim, through her daily personal prayers.

May their *neshamot* rest in Gan Eden.
*Jacky, Laurence, Elsa, Meir,
Ariel and David Cohen*

CHAPTER THREE

The *Hillula*

Asjen[1]

THIRTY FAMILIES INHABITED THE VILLAGE OF ASJEN, IN WHICH ONE can still see the ruins of an ancient Jewish quarter. It is identified by the colors the Jews had chosen to paint their houses. Most

קבר
רבי חיים
בן דיואן
זצוק״ל

The burial place of Rabbi Haim Ben Diwan. Rav Yosef
Levi is on the right, with the keeper of the place.

---

1. This article was written by Mr. Yaakov Elhadad, a journalist in Casablanca, and translated into Hebrew by Mr. Moshe Dahan.

Jews there were artisans who produced useful items for farmers. The sheriff, head of a Sunnite dynasty, had given to the Jewish community a piece of land in which to bury its dead. This site became the Jewish cemetery of the community of Ouazzane, and remains so until today. Rabbi Amram is buried in this cemetery.

Thirty years after Rabbi Amram's death, the Jewish community of Asjen was ordered to move to Ouazzane, to the innkeepers' quarter, the *mellah*. All the laws of the *dhimmi* would be applied to the community, as a minority protected by the sheriff. Before they left Asjen, the Jews put a permanent guard at the cemetery. Since Rabbi Amram's death, the *Hevra Kadisha* members took upon themselves to bury the dead free of charge.

Rabbi Amram's Grave

People made known the presence of the Tzaddik's grave in Asjen. Three times a year, Jews would come from Ouazzane in throngs to visit his tomb, by foot or on donkeys. The *Hevra Kadisha* members related that wealthy Jews who visited were surprised to find a simple mound of earth on the Tzaddik's grave and thus decided to erect a *matzevah* in his honor. The next day, they were shocked to discover that nothing remained of it but a pile of stones. They understood that they had to obey the Tzaddik's will when he requested that there be no monument on his grave.

The pile of stones covering Rabbi Amram's grave increased every year,[2] for some have the custom to place a pebble on graves they visit. It is related that those who would come to pray at the Tzaddik's grave stood near the stone in the middle, took a pebble in hand, and made their request, beseeching Rabbi Amram to intervene for them On High. This was similar to a letter written to the Tzaddik in which the petitioner says, "If you are here, here is your small

---

2. See *Teshuot Tzaddikim* 458.

stone. If you are not here, you will see it when you come." This is why numerous stones cover the grave, for the Tzaddik is not always present near his grave in Ouazzane, but in Gan Eden. From time to time, his soul would approach his grave and find the stone as if it were a letter sent to him. The Tzaddik would then give an answer in a dream himself or through a messenger.

The men who blessed and prayed for the sick, the infirm, the deaf, the childless women, and the dumb related that the Tzaddik performed miracles not only for Jews but also for Arabs who believed that he could cure the sick. Many Jews who had a son after years of childlessness named him Amram.

A number of Jews brought bottles of water with them to sanctify on the grave. They related that on the day of the *hillula*, when the sun was at its peak, a white dove often came to perch itself on one of the branches of the olive tree growing above Rabbi Amram's grave. It seemed to listen to the voices of the women shouting their traditional *yuyus*. Full of enthusiasm, the men began praying aloud. For people who cherish his memory, the presence of this dove symbolized the fact that the Tzaddik's soul is close to the grave.

During the *hillula*, women tied colored pieces of fabric on the tree above the grave, as a way of asking the Tzaddik to pray for them. The stones and the straps of fabric are signs that the Tzaddik's admirers came to visit his grave. Men sat around the pile of stones and sang in the Tzaddik's honor, recited Tehillim, or learned other texts. Once, two old blind people recited the whole *Idra* by heart.

They lit a fire in front of the olive tree. The flames licked the high green branches but did not scorch them. Further away, one could see a magnificent building, the synagogue of the Tzaddik full of worshippers. The pilgrims who came to pray sat under the trees, or in tents of all shapes and colors. Some families stayed there seven days to pray for sick family members. According to some, deaf and mute people came to pray at the grave and recovered. A forty-year-old mother, who had lost her sanity, recovered; it was a true miracle.

At the entrance of the cemetery, goods such as wine, beer, bread, batteries, lamps, and many candles were sold. At the nearby slaughterhouse, *shohetim* slaughtered all the sheep consumed at the *hillula*. Temporary restrooms were set up, near a well from which one could draw water for drinking and washing. Under the vines and in the nearby streets were stationed numerous private cars and buses servicing the pilgrims. Further, military tents were set up for the police officers watching over public order and directing traffic.

This *hillula* gave expression to the great faith of the Jewish people determined to keep its tradition in a world of Arab hostility.

The famous *gaon*, the tzaddik Rabbi Refael Encaoua, first chief rabbi of Morocco.

Pilgrimages[3]

Among Sephardic communities, the grave of Rabbi Amram Ben Diwan draws many pilgrims on the day of his *hillula*.

Mr. M. Halioua relates that in the 1930s, surrounding the grave were tens of thousands of pilgrims coming from Marrakesh in the south, and Ujda, Alziria, and Elkasar in Spanish Morocco. In the cemetery courtyard and in the surrounding orchards, the pilgrims

---

3. This article, published in the newspaper *Le Maroc*, was written by Mr. M. Halioua, member of the community council of the Jewish community of Sale, near Rabat. He currently lives in Be'er Sheva.

assembled hundreds of tents where they offered food and drink. The *hillula* committee also set up buildings for the pilgrims coming from far away, where they could rent rooms for a reasonable price.

One year, the *hillula* was held at the onset of Shabbat. As every year, the notables and the military heads coming to give honor to the event were greeted respectfully. A military parade took place and ended with fireworks. In the center of the activities, the olive tree planted over the grave stood majestically, its branches being licked by the fire.

A few men working on the holy site considered themselves as emissaries and servants of the Tzaddik. They were allowed to walk barefoot on the stones piled on the grave. These stones were hot and blackened by the candles thrown on them. Not far from there, men sitting in a half circle were learning *Zohar* and Mishnah, and reading Tehillim by the light of the candles or the dim lampposts. The committee head, Mr. Eliyahu Elhadad, who had organized the reception and the greeting of the government officials, escorted by many great Moroccan rabbis, approached the huge tent covered with rugs and silk cushions—the reception hall for the guests of honor—to welcome the mayor and his entourage, as well as the military commandant.

At the end of the military parade and the singing of the national anthem, the Andalusian orchestra played songs for the guests. The group of officials took their place in the tent prepared for them, alongside many members of royalty who considered it an honor to be present at the *hillula*. After partaking of the tea and the delicious cakes, they thanked Mr. Elhadad for his kind invitation and dispersed. The community president in turn thanked the officials for attending the reception. Everything took place in impeccable order.

Some people used the celebrations for their personal interests; some men walked barefoot on the hot stones, claiming they were servants of the Tzaddik and could bless the pilgrims. The entry fee provided the committee the necessary funds for these celebrations. The rabbinical council requested that all those whose behavior went against the sanctity of the place to make a concerted effort to act properly.

Son of the *gaon* Rabbi Michael Yissachar, fifth chief rabbi of Morocco.

Lag Ba'Omer[4]

I was impressed by the Lag Ba'Omer celebrations which annually attract thousands of pilgrims from various towns in North Africa to the Tzaddik's grave, where they envelop themselves in meditation and pray. The scenery surrounding the grave is one of rare beauty.

Some people would participate in the *hillula* that took place every Rosh Hodesh Elul. Every visitor would choose the way he wanted to make his presence felt, according to his wishes and his means. For some, the journey had been unpleasant, even dangerous, such as for those who traveled by night on unpaved roads. One could even hear the terror-stricken cries of fear that one's car would turn over. The eventful journey took two hours. These difficulties were experienced in good spirits, however; no pilgrim regretted making the effort.

When we arrived at Asjen, we saw thousands of pilgrims around the Tzaddik's tree near his grave. Stones of different sizes, blackened

---

4. This first-person account was written by Mrs. Abitbol to a French newspaper, in about 1940.

by soot and by the wax of the numerous lighted candles, covered the tomb.

The scene unfolding in front of us was fascinating. Large groups of pilgrims prostrated themselves on the stones and kissed them. The dense smoke rising from the large fire made by the candles scattered like a fog. Everyone searched for a place that would better allow them to view the festivities. Those privileged to touch the stones were able to after begging people standing in the first row to let them approach the holy site.

For some, it was their first visit to this holy place. The old-timers were deeply moved by the presence of newcomers, to whom they described the miracles they witnessed in previous years: "We have seen with our own eyes miracles happening at the grave of the Tzaddik! Not only we, but thousands of believers have seen deaf people recover their hearing, blind people who suddenly could see, and mute beginning to stammer and gradually recover their speech."

They told of a deaf and mute child who had been pushed into the fire and had tried to escape from the overheated stones. He was near death when he started to speak and to hear what the pilgrims told him. He started screaming. People forced him to repeat after them: "*Viva Rabbi Amram!*" They did not let up until he pronounced those words.

Men who doubted the Tzaddik's power to cure the unwell started being convinced of the truth of the stories they had heard. The skeptics would certainly become part of the multitude that made the yearly pilgrimage to the grave.

The Burning Bush Is Not Consumed[5]

In his last moments on earth, the Tzaddik asked the *Hevra*

---

5. These stories were related by elderly men. Mr. Moshe Dahan was an eyewitness.

The burial site of the tzaddik
Rabbi Amram Ben Diwan.

Kadisha of Asjen to lay him to rest under the olive tree. Since a road was built leading to the grave, worshippers arrive in throngs, by bus, car, or donkey. The worshippers who come to prostrate themselves on the grave of the Tzaddik light candles; many throw their lighted candles on the pile of stones covering the grave, for the elevation of the soul of the Tzaddik. The candles burn and form a huge flame.

From 1934 to 1936, visitors would enthusiastically throw candles on the Tzaddik's grave. Generous wealthy Jews from Casablanca, wanting to show their love for the Tzaddik, purchased boxes containing twenty-five packs of candles in each. When they threw them into the fire, the flames rose higher than the olive tree's peak. Candle vendors would come to the holy site with trucks full of boxes of candles. Incredibly, neither the tree's leaves nor its branches caught fire, even though the fire was so strong that the visitors had to draw back far from the grave.

Buhlal is a mountain 1,300 feet high, located in Ouazzane. It is said that from this mountain, one could clearly see the fire surrounded by smoke above Rabbi Amram's grave. A few friends and I wanted to get a look and we went up to the mountaintop. We indeed saw the fire and the smoke from five and a half miles away.

Some people could not believe that a fire so powerful did not burn the tree, so they added more candles. Not only was the tree not consumed, it remained green and fresh. It bore fruit every year, and continues to do so today! Agronomists estimated this tree to be four hundred years old, whereas the Tzaddik was buried there over two hundred years ago. Its fruit works wonders, curing people with eye ailments or other maladies as soon as they drink the juice of its olives.

Women who could not make the pilgrimage to the grave of the Tzaddik gave their neighbors strips of cloth to tie on the tree branches there. It was a message that declared, "Even though I did not come to your grave, dear Rabbi Amram, please consider it as if I did. This piece of cloth, taken from my clothes, testifies that I believe in your prayers to G-d to intercede on behalf of all those who turn to you and on behalf of the Jewish people."

The Dove: Man's Soul

Numerous pilgrims attest to seeing a dove circling above the grave of Rabbi Amram Ben Diwan. It would appear during the *hillula*, when the enthusiasm and joy were at their peak. Either shouting or whispering, the pilgrims would then ask the Tzaddik to pray for them before the Creator that their requests be answered in his merit.

After midnight, when goodness and mercy reign in the world, the dove hovered over the grave once again, indicating that the Tzaddik's soul rested on that place and prayed on their behalf.

This allusion is mentioned in the *Zohar* (*Parashat Vayakhel* 198b),

From left to right: The king of Morocco, Muhammad V, who greeted the *rabbanim* of Morocco; the famous *gaon*, the tzaddik Rabbi Shaul ibn Denan, the fourth chief rabbi of Morocco; the *gaon* Rabbi Maimon Ohayon, chief rabbi of Rabat, the capital of Morocco; followed by Avraham Drai, chief of the Jewish community of Rabat.

presented here according to the translation by the *Sulam*: "A dove comes down on a ship; it is man's soul coming down in this world to rest in his body."

Why is the soul called a dove? Because after being associated with the body, it is similar to a dove in this world. In addition, a dove hovering over a place shows that the *Shechinah* rests on that place and that prayer is accepted before the Creator. For the word *yonah* (dove) has the numerical value of 71, as does the *Shem Havayah* (*peshutah umeleah*).[6] (The *Shem Havayah* has the numerical

---

6. See the Arizal's commentary on *Shir Hashirim* (2:14), *My dove in the cracks of the rock*, that the Divine Name has the same numerical value as the word *yonah*.

value of 26 and the Divine Name has the numerical value of 45.) The *Zohar* and the Sages support this ancestral tradition.

"Happy are the tzaddikim and happy are those who cling to them!" (*Midrash Tanchuma, Vayera*).

Birds of Song[7]

The first Jewish inhabitants of Asjen had buried Rabbi Amram in 1782. Thirty years later, this community was ordered to abandon its village and reestablish itself in Ouazzane. The old men of the village related that each year, during the Tzaddik's *hillula*, doves appeared after midnight and circled the burial place.

Some say that the Tzaddik took the form of a dove. Since then, Rabbi Amram became famous and his grave became a pilgrimage site. As miracles occurred to those who revered his memory, the number of pilgrims coming from all over Morocco grew. The Tzaddik's name also became known to Algerian Jews. On the night of his *hillula*—whether sunny or rainy—a multitude of pilgrims came to pray at the holy grave. All those who prostrated themselves on Rabbi Amram's tomb came at midnight to read the *Idra* or chapters of *Tehillim*.

Before dawn, many of them began singing. At that moment, many doves appeared as if to join in the *hillula*. The pilgrims gathered around the grave, some singing, some dancing, for they felt that the Tzaddik's soul was within one of those doves. The appearance of the doves ignited ebullient enthusiasm among the crowd.

One night, at the height of the rejoicing, the doves appeared suddenly and circled the olive tree. One of the visitors was not

---

7. Yeshua Amram Bettan, president of the *Hevra Kadisha* of Ouazzane, told the following story to Hacham Shalom Israel.

convinced that when the doves come, one could pray and ask the Tzaddik to intervene On High so that G-d would cure the sick. He stared disapprovingly at the birds and muttered, "Those doves should stop flying! Aren't they tired already?"

As soon as this skeptic displayed his displeasure, the doves fell on the ground, lifeless. That year, no one benefited from a miracle and no sick person believing in Rabbi Amram Ben Diwan's powers was cured.

"The upright will live by his faith."

Viva Amram![8]

The sanctity of the gravesite was carefully preserved by the *hillula* participants. Whoever peeked inside the pilgrims' tents could hear songs of joy coming out of the visitors' mouths, sometimes even in Spanish. Slaughtered sheep hung over the tents' entrances. The smell and the smoke of barbecues rose from every corner.

According to some, the sheep slaughtered in honor of the Tzaddik had been fed for a year and were designated especially for the day of the *hillula*. Some people even brought sheep from far away, with the hope of slaughtering it in honor of the Tzaddik.

Numerous tents offering various services were stationed at the site: firefighters, paramedics, and numerous gendarmes, very impressed by the splendid spectacle. The place resembled the Garden of Eden, dotted by fruit trees whose scents blended with the aromas of roasted meat. Arak and rum flowed freely. Every visitor received a portion of meat and a cup of rum, with the prerequisite to bless the Creator in a loud voice. In this extraordinary place surrounded by mountains, the atmosphere was full of faith and trust in G-d.

Many participants stayed until midnight around the pile

---

8. This article was written by Mr. Elazar Konki.

of stones on top of the Tzaddik's grave. Suddenly, they started singing in chorus and shouting *yuyus*. Men and women raised their eyes, waiting to see the dove. When it appeared on the treetop, it stretched its wings and looked around, appearing fearful—or joyous? The pilgrims then cried out, with tears or with outstretched arms, "*Viva Rabbi Amram! Viva Rabbi Amram!*" The crowd was in high spirits, sensing the Tzaddik's soul hovering above them. The pilgrims considered the dove as Rabbi Amram's revelation in this holy site.

The onlookers were stricken by fear and seized by a strong emotion. It was only when the dove flew away that the visitors returned to their tents or their rooms. Thousands of people without accommodations spent the night under the stars. Early the next morning, they went down to the springs to wash up and cool down.

The view was splendid, and numerous trees and orchards added a pleasant and holy atmosphere. Some had made this yearly pilgrimage for dozens of years. When they took leave from one another, they blessed each other to meet again many times to celebrate the *hillula* of Rabbi Amram.

This is how they applied the verse *Ve'ahavta et Hashem Elokecha*—"You will love the Almighty, your G-d." Here, the word *et* comes to include Torah scholars.

In the center, Yosef Amram, president of the committee of holy places, in the company of *rabbanim*.

The *Hillula* Meal[9]

The *hillula* of Rabbi Amram Ben Diwan, the Hevron emissary in Morocco, is celebrated on 15 Av by a large crowd not only on his grave in Ouazzane, but in every place where Moroccan Jews live. In Ashdod, his *hillula* is celebrated each year in the house of Yitzhak Amor, one of the Tzaddik's admirers.

In the late 1990s, a bareheaded young man appeared at Yitzhak's house during the *hillula*. He asked the host for permission to explain the reason he came without an invitation. After the man was given permission to speak, he said the following:

"You see, I'm not religious. I grew up estranged from Judaism and, of course, without faith in the righteous men. I studied to be a tour guide. I was offered a job in Morocco, and for a few years I've been accompanying groups to this country. Last year, during our trip to Ouazzane, we went to the grave of Rabbi Amram Ben Diwan.

"We arrived in Asjen at twilight. Because of the residents' hostility, I gave up the visit to the Arab village and brought the group straight to the Tzaddik's grave by a roundabout road. When we arrived at the cemetery, an old woman was waiting for us. She addressed me as the leader of the group and said, 'Welcome to the grave of Rabbi Amram. I invite you to a meal.'

"We followed her, astonished. When we came into the room, we were amazed to see richly dressed tables, true to the best Moroccan tradition. When I asked her about it, the woman explained, 'This week, Rabbi Amram Ben Diwan appeared to me in a dream. He told me, "A group of forty tourists will come from Israel and they will be in danger. Quick, prepare a beautiful meal for them. By this

---

9. This story was told by Rabbi Uri Elnecave from Jerusalem, who heard it from his brother Yoel.

merit, they will be saved." This is why I hurried from Casablanca to serve you this meal.'

"We were indeed forty people, very surprised and very pleased, in particular because I had sensed the Arab villagers' enmity toward us. For the first time in my life, I found myself facing a phenomenon that I could not explain. It was certainly the power of the tzaddikim and their influence after death."

Rabbi Aharon Monsonego, sitting at the center of the burial
site of Rabbi Amram on the day of the *hillula*.
Author of this work standing next to him.

When the young man concluded his words, the host kissed him and invited him to the meal. At the end, he asked the guide to come back every year to the *hillula*.

What greatness! Not only are tzaddikim called alive after their death, but they reveal their influence to Jews estranged from their heritage and bring them closer to Judaism.

During my visit to Ouazzane in 1995, I felt a strong emotion and an indescribable holiness. I have no doubt that the qualities, holiness, and behavior of tzaddikim can produce such towering personalities as Rabbi Amram Ben Diwan!

The Reception[10]

Moroccan government officials would honor the memory of the Tzaddik by taking part in a military parade. The following *hachamim* attended this reception: Rabbi Refael Baruch Toledano, president of the rabbinical court of Meknes; and Rabbi Eliyahu Malka, chief rabbi and *dayan* of Ouazzane. The parade of the troops, wearing white coats and long swords at their belts, took place at five o'clock in the afternoon.

The attending officials were Colonel Budlai De Barzo, district military chief; the Ouazzane pasha Ali ben Kasam; his assistant sheriff Si Mahmed bal Hasam; the commandant of the town of Kiks; Captain Dufray, commissary of the sheriff's government; Mr. Jourdain, head of municipal services; Mr. Britolat, assistant to the mayor; district chief physician Robert Kitan, head of the military hospital; Abbot Lancel, priest of Ouazzane; Dr. Comet, physician; Mr. and Mrs. Lansery, diplomatic representatives in the American Consulate of Casablanca; Mr. Pinhas, headmaster of the Alliance Israelite schools, representative and secretary of the committee of Moroccan communities, with his wife; Mr. Comte, secretary and representative of the Mesed institution; the kadi Lesri, governor of the Asjen district; Mr. Bourriquet, colonel of the souabe division and his wife, the only division in which Jews were allowed to enroll; Captain Kavadinot, head of the district bureau of the town military authorities; Captain Conored, head

10. Mr. M. Halioua, head of the Jewish committee of Sala, wrote this article.

of first aid and supervision services for the protection of nature and meat roasters coming to Asjen; Commissary Quirvève, police chief and supervisor of public security; Brigadier Troyer Mervat, supervisor of the brigade and supervisor of public order in the district and of the meat roasters who came to the *hillula*.

During this magnificent reception in a huge tent, Jewish community president Mr. Eli Elhadad and the women from the community committee served mint tea and cake. Mr. Elhadad thanked all the officials for having accepted his invitation. Before they left, the guests expressed their heartfelt thanks for the kind invite. Some hurried to return home, others went to watch the pilgrims settling, and still others went to watch the fire and the crowd near the olive tree.

The Atmosphere at the *Hillula*[11]

The Jewish tradition marks the thirty-third day of the Omer count not only as the *hillula* of Rabbi Shimon bar Yohai in Meron (in Eretz Yisrael) but as many other *hillulot* to the memory of holy men from oriental countries.

On Lag Ba'Omer, thousands of people go on pilgrimage to the graves of holy men, famous *hachamim* who were miracle workers. They would spend an entire day, week, or a few weeks to pray there, joining the festivities. Sometimes, even believing non-Jews would join these *hillulot*.

Many stories are told about miracles performed by tzaddikim or by their merit. On Lag Ba'Omer, the expanse surrounding the grave of Rabbi Amram Ben Diwan became a place of rejoicing; tents covered the nearby field. One could witness heart-rending

---

11. This description by Mr. Avraham Elmaliah was first published in the newspaper *Hed Hamizrah* in Jerusalem, on 16 Iyar 5706 (May 7, 1946).

episodes, such as sick people sitting on the pile of stones with the faith that the Tzaddik would cure them. They would kindle many candles and throw them into the tall fire. Smoke scattered and covered the entire place.

To the grave of the Tzaddik came paralytics and incurable ill people, childless women, unmarried women, and deaf and mute people. They all stood near his tomb as they waited the Tzaddik's deliverance, expecting his presence to cure them.

The grave of the Tzaddik in Asjen was holy for Muslims too, as well as for their wives and children. They went to prostrate themselves on his tomb and prayed with abundant tears for their own recovery.

Asjen is a mountainous village at a distance from the town of Ouazzane. Every Jew who made the pilgrimage to join the *hillula* was considered praiseworthy. The poor and the wretched would gather money all year round to see for themselves the miracles performed in the merit of the holy Tzaddik. One year in the 1940s, over twenty thousand people made the trip!

The sight at the *hillula* on Lag Ba'Omer was awesome and splendid, as if a village had sprung from the earth for eight days. Thousands of tents covered the surrounding land.

The meat roasters brought slaughtered chicken and lambs as well as leather bottles of wine and arak for the *seudot* (feasts). The central square looked like a large fair, with its restaurants and its cafés, its microphones and amplifiers that broadcast oriental melodies and military marches.

The high point was the lighting of a huge fire, whose flames rose very high in the sky and whose smoke covered everything.

Groups of tents were set aside for the police, the doctors, and first aid. Most of the participants stayed around the grave surrounded by high trees. From afar, one could see the high mountains.

People would throw entire crates of candles into the fire. Some people took off their shoes and walked on the stones blackened by smoke. Old men in long black coats poured out their supplications, accompanying them with wide hand movements. We also saw distressed women telling their tales of woe and opening their hearts in front of the grave. Frail, sick people and men overburdened by affliction crowded together around the tomb and prayed in low voices. Infirm men suffering from all kinds of sicknesses, young and old, would come to ask for a cure.

In a corner, a young woman entreated in a low voice in front of the Hevron Tzaddik; she asked him to intercede On High for her to bear a child. A young woman having returned to a proper way of life put her forehead on the hot black stones and, crying, asked G-d to forgive her sins, for she is full of faith that her prayer will be answered.

The large and diverse crowd—a porter wearing a black tarbush, a stout merchant, a well-dressed young man, an old bearded man wearing a traditional garb—enthusiastically threw candles in the fire.

From every corner, shouts and calls, entreaties and requests resonated: "Rabbi Amram! Rabbi Amram! Cure us! *Tzaddik yesod olam*, deliver all the sick of your people! Come bring us relief! Have pity on us and deliver us!"

Many read the *Zohar* and the *Idra*. All the paralytics, the blind, and the sick lay on the stones all night. They asked the women to shout their *yuyus* and to believe that the sick would be cured, with G-d's help, in the merit of the Tzaddik. At dawn, the news of miracles having occurred at night became known. Terminally ill people were cured, the mute started to speak, old women became younger, an unbalanced woman got out of her indolence and came back to her senses, paralyzed boys on whom they spread melted wax from the candles could use their legs and begin to dance and sing, a blind man started seeing and calling people by their names, childless people have a child a year later, and so on.

All the sick who recovered blessed G-d with song. The thousands of participants ate good food offered by the families of those who were saved from their troubles. The sound of violin resonated far away.

The sums of money collected from the entrance fee and the sale of concessions in the area, which amounted to thousands of francs, were distributed to Sephardic communities in Jerusalem (in earlier years, also in Hevron).

The French government encouraged these activities, which constituted a source of development and affluence for the town of Ouazzane.

These impressive sights of the *hillula* of Rabbi Amram Ben Diwan created the beauty of the village of Asjen.

Raphael Ouknine (left), director of the school of the Alliance of
Mogador, Beni-Mellal, Port Lyautey, Ouazzane, and Rabat.
To the right, Chief Rabbi Ovadia Yosef is visiting
one of the schools that he founded in France.

Entrance of the cemetery.

This chapter is dedicated in loving memory of
Rabbi Rephael Ohayon *a"h*

May the memory of Rabbi Rephael Ohayon *a"h* be a
source of inspiration through this book, amen.

Mrs. Simy Ohayon
Manuel and Shani Kanner and Family
Yehuda and Rena Azoulay and Family
Esther Borgese and Family

Le'ilui Nishmat
Ribi David Kadoch *a"h*

who taught us how to live a life dedicated to Torah,
Tefillah, *Hesed* and *Abodat Hashem*

"First for all matters of holiness"

Yossi and Ashlene Azulay and Children

This chapter is dedicated in loving memory of my dear mother
Raquel Benhaim *zt"l*

Moshe Benhaim

CHAPTER FOUR

Miracles

Saved from Drowning[1]

IT IS WEDNESDAY, AUGUST 9, 2006 (15 MENACHEM AV 5766), AND
I am on my way to pray Shaharit at six in the morning at the Syrian
synagogue in Tel Aviv, near Ben Yehuda Street. My brother-in-
law Marc Dayan, who is spending his vacation with us, is at my
side. When we leave the synagogue at seven, I suggest to Marc that
we go immerse ourselves at the beach. He agrees to come with me.

We go back to the hotel to take our towels and then set out
for the beach to the right of the Hilton Hotel in Tel Aviv. The
beach, totally deserted, has no post for lifeguards. In this lovely
creek, the sea is calm, splendid. We go down to the water from the
left side of the creek near the boulders, up to our shoulders, then
immerse ourselves one after the other. Marc dips first and when

---

1. This story was told by Josué (Yeshua Amram) Bettan, who lives in Paris. He
   is a grandson of Yeshua Amram Bettan, president of the *Hevra Kadisha* "Rabbi
   Shimon bar Yohai" in Ouazzane, and of Yosef Amram, president of the holy site
   of the tzaddik Rabbi Amram Ben Diwan.

he is finished, it is my turn. Our immersion takes fifteen minutes at most.

When he lifts his head from the water, Marc tells me that he thinks that we will not be able to go back to shore. At first, I think it's a bad joke. Then I realize that the water is rough, the sea has risen, and we are far from shore. I understand that he is not joking.

I answer him, "No way! We'll swim back!"

We thus swim toward shore. Long minutes fly by. The more we swim, the further we find ourselves. We see from a distance the first people arriving at the beach. They seem to us as minuscule dots. We begin to make hand signs, to shout, but we have to admit that nobody hears us. We are too far from the coast.

I come up with the idea to get close to the boulders and then climb on them. I signal to Marc and we try to get closer. We quickly come to the realization that it is much too dangerous; the water dashes on the rocks so violently that we would be crushed against them. We swim against the current far from the rocks.

We begin to lose our strength. A month earlier, I had undergone a surgery from which I had not completely recovered. I cannot withstand the effort.

Marc whispers that he cannot go on and that he is going to drown.

I tell him, "No way! We must go on!"

I place my left arm around his right arm and I swim as I can, lifting him out of the water. I say to myself that going to immerse in the sea was my idea in the first place, and that I must absolutely bring my friend back safe and sound. This stimulates me and gives me new vigor to swim, still helping Marc maintain his head out of the water.

The current is very strong and drives us further away from the beach. We dabble about all the time to float on the surface, using up our strength.

I begin seeing the truth—we cannot return to shore and the people on the beach do not see us. Soon we will go under from exhaustion. I start shivering from cold; I have no more strength. And I say to myself that it is silly to die there, a few hundred feet from the beach, when our families are still sleeping and that when they get up they will hear that we drowned. Slowly, I get colder and colder.

Suddenly, I feel that my arm no longer holds Marc's. I turn my head and see him sinking. Then his head reappears. He tells me that he can hold on no longer and he goes under. I do not see him anymore. I look for him a long time but he does not reappear. I understand that he drowned. In a blur, I ask myself how I can come back without him and tell my sister that he died.

Then I realize that I myself cannot keep my head out of the water. I have no more strength. The beach is very far, the sea very strong, and I cannot keep my head out of the water. I understand that I am going to die. I begin swallowing my first gulps of salted water. I say to myself that I can let myself sink just a second to rest and regain strength; it's like when one is very sleepy and thinks that he needs just a short nap to feel better. I thus sink for the first time, close to the surface. I lift my head out of the water, I don't know how. I think that I cannot go on and that I am going to drown for real.

Suddenly, I do not know from where, a cry bursts from inside me.

I yell, "Rabbi Amram Ben Diwaaaaaaaaaaaaaaaaaaaan!"

And in a second, the miracle happens!

Marc emerges from the water as a rocket taking off. His torso is entirely out of the water, up to his hips, totally erect. Then he turns around, places himself closer to the beach, and floats on the water.

For my part, I find an unexpected energy; I do not know from where it comes. The sea immediately becomes calm, similar to a pond. I feel held up by an invisible hand and deposited in the water behind Marc. In this position, Marc is first and makes calm breaststrokes. My hands on his shoulders, I progress by moving my feet.

We thus swim slowly, Marc in front and me behind, stuck together in tranquil waters. Each of us feels an extraordinary, miraculous internal tranquility, as well as the strength to progress slowly to shore.

After a while, we hear shouts around us and we see lifeguards coming toward us in a boat and on surfboards. The lifeguard on the surfboard attends to us. He asks us to take hold of his surfboard and to move our feet, as he pulls us with a rope to the shore. He calls to us without letup and taps with the palm of his hand on the surfboard.

He shouts at us, "Why did you swim so far? Why?" We do not understand why he obstinately lectures us in deep water, but we understand it later on. We were far from the shore, extenuated and frozen, and he was mainly trying to keep us awake.

We arrive near the beach. The lifeguard lifts Marc, who is in a very bad shape, and drags him to shore to put an oxygen mask on him. He tells me, "Walk up to the sand."

This is when the second miracle happens. I am in water that is two feet deep and I let go of the surfboard. I try to stand to walk to the beach, but my legs no longer hold me. I collapse in those two feet of water, perfectly conscious, head into the water. I had seen that everybody was surrounding Marc and that no one was looking in my direction.

I say to myself, *Isn't it foolish to drown a few feet away from the beach?* I make an immense effort to roll on my back. I succeed by a miracle and lift my head out of the water. Then I crawl on my back until I get out of the water.

We remain on the sand for a long time. Then, after we regain our strength, we leave the beach, a Psalm on our lips: *"From the depth of my distress I called the Almighty and He answered me..."*[2]

Marc is taken to the hospital that same day. I return home. I was later told that for three days, I hovered between life and death, burning with fever and prostrated, especially with the sensation that my left foot was pulled to make me go under. On Shabbat night, the third day after my accident, I remembered King David, who, to prolong his days, read *Tehillim* the whole Shabbat. I thus got up in the dead of night and I slowly read *Tehillim* until dawn. Then I was taken to the hospital.

The most interesting thing is that I learned that the day of the almost-drowning was 15 Av, the day people celebrate the *hillula* of Rabbi Amram Ben Diwan all over the world. The tzaddik Rabbi Amram Ben Diwan had interceded On High to save us. We benefited from numerous miracles to escape death: Marc came out alive from the deep water, even though he had remained submerged for a long time; both of us regained our strength; the sea became quiet after being tumultuous; we were placed in a position that allowed us to swim while we waited for help; the lifeguards from another beach were called in time and came to us despite the very high waters (as they told us); I succeeded in removing myself from the two-foot high water, and came out healthy from the three-day fight for my life.

In fact, we stayed in the water much more than a few minutes,

---

2. *Tehillim* 118:5.

as we had originally thought. We went into the water at 7:20 and came out at 10:25. We had thus remained in the sea for three hours and five minutes! What a miracle!

Years later on that beach, we met a man whom we had seen on that fateful day in August. He told us that he had spotted us when we were in the water. He called for help, and the lifeguards had to fight hard to arrive near us. According to him, we were at the most dangerous place of the creek, where the water came back to the deep sea with a violent return of the waves, and we had no way of coming out alive. He, too, acknowledged that we survived by a miracle.

A few years ago, improvements were made to the beach: bathing is forbidden in the entire left part, which is now roped off, and a lifeguard post was set up.

May Rabbi Amram Ben Diwan's merit protect every Jew, wherever he is.

"*Viva Rabbi Amram Ben Diwan! Viva!*"

The Double Miracle[3]

The following episode, which took place during World War II, became known to all Ouazzane Jews. They heard it from trustworthy people who were present near Rabbi Amram Ben Diwan's grave at the time.

The wealthy Corcos family from Tangiers owned several pharmacies. One of those pharmacies was run by one of their sons, a certified pharmacist. Unfortunately, he was stricken by polio when he was thirty, and his two legs became paralyzed. The young man's infirmity deprived his family of all joy; his parents'

---

3. Mr. Moshe Dahan heard this story from eyewitnesses and from the *Hevra Kadisha* members who prayed for the sick man.

worry and distress grew from day to day, for they had consulted with every expert, as far as in France and Spain, who did not give their son the slightest hope of recovery.

Despite their suffering, the man's parents did not despair. His father was very religious and had brought up his sons with strong faith in G-d. They heard about the grave of a tzaddik drawing thousands of pilgrims to the cemetery of the Arab village of

A painting of the tzaddik Rabbi Amram Ben Diwan, G-d bless his memory.

Asjen. People encouraged them to bring their son to the grave and to spend at least eight days there. It was reported that a sick person who stayed seven days near the Tzaddik's grave was assured Divine help and a miracle in the Tzaddik's merit. He could even be cured during his stay.

Mr. Corcos phoned Mr. Eli Elhadad, whose wife was related to the Corcos family from Mogador. He explained his plans to go for a few days with his family to the Tzaddik's grave. He asked Mr. Elhadad to organize a *minyan* to pray with them, a *hazan*, a *shohet* (ritual slaughterer), a butcher, and household help, as well as a few rooms in Mr. Yosef Amram's private building.

Because of their social status and their relationships with the Christian and Spanish societies, the Corcos family had asked the organizers to keep their pilgrimage a secret. The *minyan* members, the men learning Torah, the *shohet*, and the *hazan* all fulfilled their roles inconspicuously and humbly. A kind of retreat was arranged for them, complete with everything they would need. Two *minyanim* of *Hevra Kadisha* members arrived in Asjen and began praying.

A man was responsible for buying food, which was abundant. He went daily into town to buy sheep and all the supplies. Under a tall olive tree, the butcher set up a place to slaughter the animals. The cooks brought their pots, and the *shohet* prepared to slaughter a large ox. Every day, he would slaughter sheep and distribute the meat to the poor and to the men learning Torah.

When the *shohet* was ready to slaughter the ox—considered an offering for the merit of the tzaddik Rabbi Amram, but in fact it was a thanksgiving gift to G-d—women would bring drums, and others would adorn the ox's head with shining colored material, tie kerchiefs around its neck, put gold bracelets around its horns, and cover it with a cloth.

Whoever saw this joyous sight accompanied by songs in honor of the Tzaddik could not imagine that this ox would be slaughtered so that, by the Tzaddik's merit, G-d would perform a miracle and cure the sick man. Mr. Corcos was on the one hand sad for his sick son, and on the other hand delighted by the ray of hope that had appeared. He stood up and announced, "If my son recovers, I'll come every year to slaughter an ox and distribute its meat to the poor!"

During the eight-day visit, the Corcos son joined the group three times a day in the prayers and in the study of *Zohar*, *Tehillim*, and *Idra*. All the reading and study was of course held in the synagogue of the Tzaddik.

Suddenly, one night at midnight, as they stood to pray at Rabbi Amram's grave, the paralyzed young man stood and walked unaided to the grave! The crowd's joy was indescribable, especially Mr. Corcos's! Everyone began singing the song about Rabbi Amram, "Rabbi Amram Ben Diwan is sitting at the Heavenly Yeshiva..."

At the entrance of the synagogue close to the Tzaddik's burial place.

A few days after the young Corcos's recovery, the group started to disperse. Mr. Corcos distributed money generously. It was only afterwards that the news of the miracle became known. Many friends of Mr. Corcos, as well as a crowd of inquisitive people, came to the grave of the Tzaddik to see the miracle for themselves. The joy was at its peak: the young man sat, his back to the holy ark, while the crowd sang songs about the Tzaddik. Mr. Corcos distributed large sums to the poor at this time. A few hours later, the Corcos family left the cemetery. They bade farewell to those who shared their joy, with good wishes, blessings, and tears.

However, the story does not end here, as Mr. Corcos had vowed that if his son recovered, he would slaughter an ox every year for the merit of Rabbi Amram Ben Diwan and would distribute its meat to the poor. Due to his various activities, Mr. Corcos forgot his vow and did not bring an ox the following year. A year later, his son began feeling his legs weaken from day to day. The doctors who examined him saw a regression; they said that his paralysis could very well come back.

Searching his memory, Mr. Corcos suddenly understood the connection between his son's relapse and his oversight. It is said that the family secretly went back to the holy site and asked for forgiveness. After that, their son was completely cured.

The Tzaddik certainly does not need people to eat and drink at his grave. After his death, he is concerned that one should feed the numerous poor who visit the cemetery. In the merit of a generous vow made by a man, the Tzaddik prays on his behalf and G-d answers his request.

May his merit protect us!

From Casablanca to Asjen[4]

In 1974 in Ouazzane, a young Jew from Casablanca was stricken by an Arab police officer. The blow was so strong that the boy fell backwards. At the hospital, the doctors said his spinal column was severely damaged and they pronounced him paralyzed in both legs.

No bus driver agreed to carry the wounded boy lying on a stretcher on his bus together with other passengers to the Tzaddik's grave. This boy's mother, a widow crushed by the tragedy, had neither the energy nor the means to hire a private taxi to Asjen for her son. Distressed by the woman's suffering, a neighbor of hers

---

4. This story appears in *Ha'aratzat Hakedoshim.* The Arab guard Lachsen tells it to the visitors coming to the holy grave.

named Habib decided to take the boy there on a donkey. He bought a strong donkey at the market, set the young man in a double basket (*svari* in Arabic), and transported him on the animal.

Habib set out on foot, the donkey at his side. The paralyzed young man sat in one of the baskets, and in the other, to counterbalance his weight, Habib put all sorts of items. This is how, out of pity for the poor widow, Habib walked from morning to night, spending the nights in Arab villages where the inhabitants took pity on the sick young man and his devoted attendant.

Eliyahu Amram Elhadad, last president of the community.

In some villages, a few Jewish families offered them food and drink. The trip lasted ten days, during which Habib cared for the boy with endless devotion.

When they finally arrived at the Asjen cemetery, Habib placed the young man at the foot of the olive tree. He entreated the old men who walked on the stones to pray for the unfortunate boy, explaining his predicament. "Please, consider him as an offering before G-d and pray for his cure!"

Habib heard the young man whispering, "Rabbi Amram Hatzaddik! See my mother's suffering and cure me! And if not, take back my soul, for I prefer death to such a life!"

Habib was so tired that he fell asleep in spite of the songs and the prayers recited by the pilgrims. When he woke up, he stood guard in front of the boy the whole night.

The pilgrims who visited Rabbi Amram's grave every year on Lag Ba'Omer said that it is recommended to pray and beseech G-d, to call the Tzaddik and ask for his help, at two moments. One can pray either at midday or at midnight when the dove perches on the olive tree, or when a snake appears on the tree and on the black stones covering the grave, which always occurs.

The first night following Habib and the young boy's arrival, nothing occurred. The paralyzed young man moaned the whole night due to his distress and suffering. The second night, after Lag Ba'Omer, an unusual thing happened before the old men who distributed holy water poured from the bottles which remained all night between the stones on the grave. A little snake scurried between the young man's feet, which began moving. The old men began screaming for joy, "*Yuyu! Viva Rabbi Amram!*" A few men seized the boy and helped him walk around Rabbi Amram's tree. He painfully stood up, but could move his legs. What a miracle!

The happiest bystander was Habib. It was thanks to his initiative that the young man could stand! The news about the miracle spread quickly and people came out of every tent to see the young man. The songs and the dances took place until morning.

After praying Shaharit, the pilgrims reluctantly left the holy site.

Day by day, the young man recovered the use of his legs. He and Habib did not go back home on a donkey; they remained at the site to help the Arab guard Lachsen, until some visitors took them to Casablanca in their car.

The Gravedigger's Prayer[5]

In Morocco, particularly in Ouazzane, there was an ancient custom that when a boy became bar mitzvah, his parents would

---

5. Mr. Moshe Dahan remembers this event, which took place during his youth.

train him to volunteer with the *Hevra Kadisha*. Before the burial of an elderly man, the *Hevra Kadisha* members, including the vice president, would let the young boy into the open grave. All the men in attendance, including the boy's father, distributed drinks to the *Hevra Kadisha* members and toasted *lehaim*. The vice president would then declare, "By your merit, Rabbi Shimon bar Yohai, protect this boy and may he be a volunteer for many years in this group bearing your name!" The boy would lie on his back in the grave for one second and then stand and come out. From that day on, he was a volunteer of the *Hevra Kadisha*, until his last day.

When his turn came to serve in the *Hevra Kadisha*, he was given a task according to his abilities, which he could not refuse. If his age allowed him to lift the coffin, he had to do that.

At the end of the town was an open area called "the place of the coffin," where they called the men who would carry the coffin five and a half miles, from the town to the cemetery. If the body was heavy, twelve volunteers were called upon; three groups of four took turns carrying the coffin on their shoulders for one and a half miles each. During this time, the gravediggers went ahead to the cemetery and began digging the grave.

If the body was that of a five-year-old child, two men would carry him in a small coffin. If the deceased was less than two years old, one man carried him on his shoulder in a basket or in a folded piece of cloth.

One day, it was the turn of a strong, brave merchant to carry a deceased little girl. He refused to pay someone to take his place—not to save money, but in order that he should perform the commandment to bury the dead. He placed the child on his shoulder and, despite the heavy rain, began walking alone. When he arrived in front of a stream whose waters had swelled, he placed the child's body on his head. He began swimming to the other edge of the stream and cried, "By your merit, Rabbi Shimon bar Yohai, author of the *Zohar*, help me! Let me come out and perform my duty!" He had faith in our Sages' saying that "a man going to perform a commandment is not harmed." He surfaced on the other bank, thoroughly drenched, and swiftly walked the three remaining miles to the cemetery.

He began digging the grave when he suddenly saw an Arab holding a gun, accompanied by his ill son. They were standing in a place where no one was allowed to stand—on the stones covering the Tzaddik's grave! The Arab pointed his gun toward the volunteer. Shaking with fright, the Jew ran to the olive tree growing over the grave and grasped it, saying, "If I must die, I prefer to die sanctifying the Divine Name and grasping Rabbi Amram's tree!"

The Arab was ready to shoot, when his hand suddenly became paralyzed. The volunteer then spotted the Arab's son sitting near the grave of the Tzaddik and understood that his father had brought him there to pray for a cure for his illness.

Stunned, the Arab could neither utter a word nor move. The *Hevra Kadisha* member turned his head in the direction of Rabbi Amram's grave and said, "My master, Rabbi Amram! Since this man did not harm me or kill me, please cure him and his son!"

At that precise moment, the Arab started to speak and move, as did his son! When he saw the sudden miracle, the Arab begged the Jew's forgiveness, saying, "I didn't know that your Tzaddik could perform such miracles!"

Back in Ouazzane, the *Hevra Kadisha* volunteer told this story to the members of his community. Used to hearing about the miracles that occurred at the grave, the Jews accepted this wonder as self-evident.

Portal next to the cemetery toward the burial site.

A Child Is Cured[6]

It was hard to reach the grave of Rabbi Amram Ben Diwan. Riding on the path was nearly impossible. The pilgrims coming on donkeys, mules, and horses, and sometimes in cars, arrived at the grave with great effort. The narrow path paved with rocks put the travelers in danger.

At one point in time, a Christian Frenchman was appointed mayor of Ouazzane. He had friendly relationships with the influential Jews of the town. Unfortunately, his only son was suffering from polio. Distressed at seeing the child suffering from this incurable illness, some Jewish and Arab friends of the mayor advised him to take his son to Rabbi Amram's grave, but he was not convinced. In the end, the mayor decided that he had nothing

---

6. This story was written by Jewish historian Mr. Elazar Konki and was disclosed by Mr. Moshe Dahan.

to lose and brought his son to the burial place of the Tzaddik, the *sied*, as the Arabs called him.

As he walked toward the grave, the mayor started praying in French and made a vow—that if a miracle occurred and his son was cured, he would pay for the building of a new road to facilitate access to the cemetery.

After a number of visits to Rabbi Amram's grave, the mayor's son started moving his legs. A year later, he was completely cured and was walking without help—a miracle! The mayor continued to visit the Tzaddik's grave a few times over the next few years. True to his word, he sponsored the building of a wide road suitable for motor vehicles to ride on. At its opening ceremony, a huge tent was erected near the grave. The mayor organized a parade and a reception for VIPs on Lag Ba'Omer, which then became a yearly tradition. He also invited the military officers of the town, the pasha, and police officers, and offered an abundance of food and drink.

The French mayor had deep faith in the Tzaddik's influence and began publicizing the holy site. After this episode became known, many new visitors joined the old-timers every year at the pilgrimage.

Blessed be G-d Who sanctifies His Name in public!

A Blind Child Recovers His Sight[7]

The old men of the town relate that during the rejoicing aroused by the appearance of the doves, a mother gave her blind son over to the worshippers standing on top of the stones. These men prayed to G-d on the child's behalf and asked all the bystanders to shout, "*Viva Rabbi Amram!* No one is as great as you, a tzaddik who

---

7. This article was written in French by Mr. Elazar Konki around 1940.

performs miracles by your prayers to G-d!" Suddenly, the child opened his eyes! The bystanders were so enthralled and so tightly packed that the child tried to flee. It was very hot near the flames. The son then saw his mother close to him and was reassured. He jumped into her arms, crying for joy, sharing with her his wonder and elation.

An old rabbi approached and spoke to the bystanders. "See, gentlemen," he said, "this child who recovered his eyesight. See this miracle!"

Some people showed the child items or clothes and asked him, "What color is this?" The child answered their questions without hesitation.

The old rabbi approached the boy, put his hand on his head, and blessed him for benefiting a miracle. He thanked G-d and blessed the child to get married during his mother's life.

Blessed be G-d Who opens the eyes of the blind.

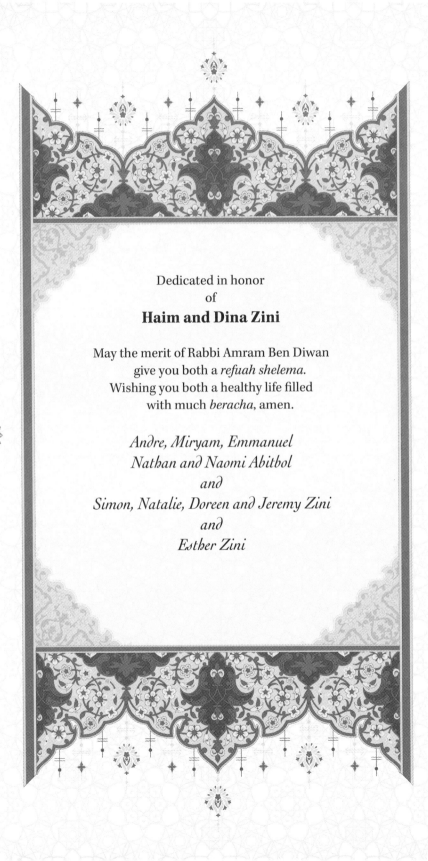

Dedicated in honor
of
Haim and Dina Zini

May the merit of Rabbi Amram Ben Diwan
give you both a *refuah shelema*.
Wishing you both a healthy life filled
with much *beracha*, amen.

Andre, Miryam, Emmanuel
Nathan and Naomi Abitbol
and
Simon, Natalie, Doreen and Jeremy Zini
and
Esther Zini

CHAPTER FIVE

Hand of G-d

The Stolen Bank

A WOMAN IN MOROCCO HAD COMPLETE FAITH IN THE MIRACLES performed by Rabbi Amram Ben Diwan. However, she was so poor that she could not afford the trip to Asjen on Lag Ba'Omer. So every day, when her husband gave her money to buy food, she would put aside a coin and drop it in a small box. She hid the box, which she called "The Money Bank of Rabbi Amram Ben Diwan," under her bed. As her husband did not encourage her to make the pilgrimage for the *hillula* of Rabbi Amram, she did not reveal the existence of this box.

Before Lag Ba'Omer, the woman went, without her husband's knowledge, to book a ticket for the trip to Asjen, which was organized from all the towns in Morocco. One night, in a dream, she saw a man, who told her, "Get up! Get up! Your money bank is empty! One of your close relatives stole its contents."

This woman had a son who would go gambling with a friend of

Front door in the middle of the *mellah*; inside was the
synagogue of Rabbi Amram Ben Diwan.

his. The two boys had found the box and decided to empty it and
use the money for gambling. The young men had gone to the club
and lost all the money.

When she woke up, the woman removed the box from its
hiding place and found it empty. She immediately called her son
and asked, "How much money did you take from the box?"

Trembling from fear and shame, the young man answered, "I…
didn't take that money. My friend emptied the box and used the
money to gamble. He lost everything."

The woman went to speak with the other boy's mother. She
explained that the stolen money was intended to pay the fare to
Asjen for the *hillula* of Rabbi Amram, and requested the money
back. The friend's mother was appalled at the thought that her son
had stolen money—money kept for the pilgrimage to the Tzaddik's

grave! Her son, however, admitted that he had taken 1,500 francs from the box, but added that the son of the other woman had taken the rest. The woman of the second boy told her husband the whole story.

This honest man understood that the poor woman had thus lost all her money—three thousand francs. Without telling her that the theft was in part perpetrated by the woman's own son, he gave her the total sum and asked her forgiveness for his son's wrongdoing.

The woman went to Asjen as she had hoped, certain that without the Tzaddik who had prayed for her On High and revealed the theft in her dream, she would not have merited to pray at his grave.

How great are the deeds of the righteous!

Solika's Illness[1]

In the 1990s, a woman named Solika became ill. The doctors at Hillel Yaffe hospital, in Hadera, said that she suffered from a malignant growth in her brain. Two years before, she suffered from memory lapses and constant dizziness. In spite of constant medical care, her condition worsened. The doctors in the neurology ward conferred with each other, asking whether they should operate, with the risks that entailed, when they knew that the prospects of cure were so flimsy. The woman's very religious and honorable family came to the drastic decision that surgery should be performed.

During the weeks of preparation and treatment before the procedure, the sick woman dreamed about a man named Amram ben Hayun (who lives today in Casablanca). All the sick woman's neighbors knew the man, who attended to the grave of Rabbi Amram and rejoiced the pilgrims by his songs in honor of the

---

1. The woman, daughter of a scholar and wife of a G-d-fearing man, herself told her story to Mr. Moshe Dahan. Today she lives with her husband in Hadera.

Tzaddik. He also blessed the people who asked for his blessing at Rabbi Amram's grave.

In her dream, Solika saw him at the hospital. He told her, "Solika! I came to take you out of here! Stand up and go out!"

She woke up, startled, and could not go back to sleep. When her husband came to visit her in the morning, she told him her dream.

From then on, her health improved. During his visits, her husband saw that Solika was feeling better. When she suggested forgoing the procedure, he was surprised and did not dare bring up this idea to the doctors.

The physicians themselves noticed the improvement in Solika's health and decided to postpone the surgery. For the time being, however, they wanted to keep her under observation in the hospital. Solika feared that the doctors would later decide to perform the procedure and insisted that her husband take her out of the hospital immediately. But before they could leave, a miracle happened— the doctors who, a few days before, wanted to perform surgery, came to tell her that she could leave the hospital.

Solika recovered completely and thanked G-d and the tzaddik Rabbi Amram who appeared in her dream in the form of Amram ben Hayun.

An Amulet on the Grave[2]

Before the United States fought in Vietnam, Indochina was a French colony. The French desperately waited for armed assistance from the Americans, but the Americans did not enter the conflict because they knew that the French could not subdue the rebels in Indochina.

---

2. Mr. Yosef Dahan, who today lives in Givat Olga, told Mr. Moshe Dahan what his aunt recounted.

Gravesite of the tzaddik Rabbi Amram Ben Diwan.

The president of the French Council, Pierre Mendès-France, obtained an armistice. Until then, fierce battles had been fought between the colonial army and the rebels, during which many French soldiers had been slain.

A Jewish woman had moved from Morocco to France. She lived near a French family whose son was sent by the army to Indochina during this bloody war. The boy's mother was very worried about her son's fate, and was happy when he returned home on a month-long furlough.

The woman's Jewish neighbor felt concerned by the danger the young soldier was exposed to in the battlefield. Every time she spoke about it with the soldier's mother, the Jewish neighbor told her, naively perhaps, to have faith in G-d and in the tzaddik Rabbi Amram Ben Diwan. The Jewish woman was convinced that the Tzaddik had performed miracles for Jews when they lived in Morocco. When Jews left Morocco, two-thirds—more than

200,000 people—left for Eretz Yisrael, and among the last third, some moved to Canada and others to France.

The Jewish woman was worried for her neighbor as if she were a family member. Nevertheless, it was hard for her to convince the Catholic woman of the Tzaddik's power.

While the soldier was still on furlough, the Jewish woman tried to persuade the soldier's mother to come with her to the Lag Ba'Omer *hillula*, to pray on the Tzaddik's grave that her son be saved from the battles in Indochina.

Finally, after hearing about all the miracles, the neighbor agreed to come with her. The Jewish woman recommended preparing an amulet from a Moroccan coin worth four francs. The women put this coin among the blackened stones above the grave while they were praying. When they came back to France, the soldier's furlough was ending. Before he returned to his base, his mother asked him to put on his neck the amulet prepared by her neighbor. She added a twenty-franc coin and asked him to never take the amulet off his neck.

During the first weeks in Indochina, the son wrote letters to his parents as much as he could. After a few months, the fighting intensified. His correspondence ceased; his mother received neither letters nor phone calls.

Faithful to his promise, the soldier always kept the amulet on his neck. During a battle, he was shot with a bullet in the chest. However, the bullet hit the coin suspended from his neck and did not hurt him. He immediately understood that the miracle happened thanks to the coin that was placed on the stones of the Tzaddik's grave.

For several months, the soldier could not contact his parents, for his unit was stationed in a deserted area. For weeks, he could not even wash and his beard grew wild.

His parents were beside themselves with worry. Did their son die in battle or disappear? It often happened that the army delayed informing the family of the loss of their dear ones quite a while after the fact, or even until the unit returned to France. Every day, the Jewish woman went to visit her neighbor to try to give her support.

One day, the parents heard a knock on the door. The mother went to open it and saw in front of her a bearded man with long hair and a dirty uniform.

"Who are you?" she asked him.

"It's me, your son! Don't you recognize me?"

The mother started crying from joy. She called her Jewish neighbor, who was very happy to see the soldier back in good health. Then the son related that he was saved from a bullet because it hit the amulet suspended from his neck without penetrating his breast.

Blessed be G-d Who sanctifies His Name in public!

The Kotel's Holiness[3]

I feel it is a great merit to tell the incredible story that happened to me on the day of the *hillula* of Rabbi Amram Ben Diwan in Ouazzane, Morocco, in 1995. I consider it a duty to make this story known, for it shows that "the tzaddikim in their death are called alive."[4] The Baal Shem Tov said that telling stories about tzaddikim is similar to learning the verses of the Torah describing the Divine Chariot. We have grown up on the pure faith conveyed by the behavior and the teachings of these saintly men.

I would like to begin by telling that my parents come from

---

3. This story was told by Rabbi Yosef Halevi, rabbi of Katzrin, Israel.

4. See *Shemuel II* 23:20.

The door of the entrance of the *mellah* of Sale. On the left there is
a monument in the name of Rabbi Amram Ben Diwan. According
to a tradition, the Tzaddik lived there, and every Saturday night the
members of the community pray and light a candle in his memory.

Morocco. I myself was born in Eretz Yisrael, but in my youth I
absorbed the culture of Moroccan Jews and their faith in Sages.

I received one day an unexpected phone call from an old friend
asking me if I was interested in joining in the *hillula* of Rabbi
Amram Ben Diwan in Morocco on Lag Ba'Omer. It was nine days
before the *hillula*, but I did not hesitate for a moment. I accepted
wholeheartedly as if I had been planning the trip for months.

My immediate positive response, without verifying in the
calendar and without consulting my family, strengthened in me
the faith that I just had to go pray at the Tzaddik's grave. My
mother, who came with me to Morocco, indeed told me, "The
Tzaddik calls you—go!"

Thank G-d, I got my passport and my ticket without undue
delay. Before leaving, I decided to offer the Tzaddik a present

from the Holy Land, the land he loved and for which he went to Morocco on a mission.

Since I had read that his grave was covered by a pile of stones, I thought that the best would be to deposit on his grave a stone from the Holy Land. I went to the Kotel (Western Wall) underground vaults, where I encountered a friend of mine who supervised the excavations. When I told him about my idea, he brought me to the site, gave me a stone, and asked for my blessing.

And there I was, standing and shaking before the grave of Rabbi Amram Ben Diwan. I saw a multitude of Jews from around the world. It was a very moving moment.

We prayed Minhah and then put on a *djellaba*, a robe, as is done in that circumstance. I took my *shehitah* tools and slaughtered five lambs. All of them were *chalak*, without any filament stuck to the lungs of the animals. I saw it as an auspicious sign.

After Arvit, we sang and recited liturgical poems. We had a meal in honor of the Tzaddik, during which we spoke *divre Torah*. We then said the *Birkat Hamazon*, the Grace after Meals. The time had come for me to put down my stone from the Holy Land.

It was around 11:00 p.m. On the pile of stones, I saw the ash of the small fires and of the candles lit in honor of the Tzaddik.

I read chapters of *Tehillim* and made a *hashkavah* in the Tzaddik's memory. I then said the verse, *He will make atonement for his land and his people*[5] and placed my stone in the middle of the pile.

Then something incredible happened.

Suddenly, a southwest wind caused a whirlwind that gathered the small fires into a large fire five feet high, exactly at the place where I had put my stone. This gust of wind whistled beautifully for a few seconds, then it broke and each fire went back to its original place. What an amazing sight!

---

5. *Devarim* 32:43.

I must admit that I was stunned. My mother told me in Arabic that the Tzaddik had taken the stone and that I should not be afraid.

Standing beside us, a young Israeli asked me if I had put some chemical product on the stone. I answered in a coarse voice that it was a stone from the underground vaults of the Kotel. He was very impressed and asked me to bless him.

My mother then took my hand and led me out of the cemetery. The men surrounding the grave had taken in what had happened and were coming to me to receive my blessing. My mother probably feared the evil eye.

This event stayed with me during my whole stay in Morocco and haunts me until today. Every time I relate it, the extraordinary whistle echoes in my ears and fills me with a feeling of holiness and spiritual elevation.

May the Tzaddik's merit protect the Jewish people!

The Holy Stone[6]

Each stone from the pile covering Rabbi Amram Ben Diwan's grave is part of the holy site. In his humility, the Tzaddik had requested, as we have seen, that no monument be erected on his grave. It was to be marked with a simple mound of stones.

In Iyar 5742/1982, I went on a tour to Morocco via Paris together with my friend Rabbi Meir Elazar Attia. After we landed in Casablanca, we took a special bus to Asjen eight days before Lag Ba'Omer. We thus visited the grave of Rabbi Amram on the first day of our visit to Morocco. We stayed there only two hours and then traveled on to Fez.

I went to Asjen a second time on Lag Ba'Omer, which was on a

_____

6. This story was told by Mr. Moshe Dahan.

Sunday. When the traditional ceremony of the *hillula* ended, very few visitors remained. It was heartrending to see there only twenty people—men, women, and children. Where were the thousands of pilgrims who used to visit the grave of Rabbi Amram Ben Diwan on Lag Ba'Omer? I stayed two nights on the grounds and on Tuesday, I was due to return to Rabat, where I was to meet Rabbi Meir Elazar Attia. Before my departure, I prayed at the graves of my grandfather, my grandmother, and my father.

As a *gabbai* of the synagogue Rabbi Amram Ben Diwan in Givat Olga (Hadera), I had the idea to take a stone from the Tzaddik's grave to be placed in the holy ark of the synagogue bearing his name.

When I asked some respected men if I could take a stone, they answered, "Beware! Don't do such a thing! It is forbidden to take even a speck of this pile!"

The *mellah* of Ouazzane (Jewish neighborhood).

I confess that I unfortunately did not listen to them. I took with me a large stone weighing about four pounds.

From that day on, I ran into some very unpleasant incidents.

The first was that when I went on the bus in Rabat, two Arabs stole my pocketbook holding all my money—a hefty sum of $1,500. In my pocketbook were also my credit card and my exit permit, the document authorizing me to fly back to Eretz Yisrael. I was left penniless, without even the means to get to the *mellah* (walled Jewish quarter) of Rabat to meet my friend Rabbi Meir Elazar Attia. I thus had to cover the distance on foot.

I am a believing man. I understood that I was punished for having taken a stone from the grave of Rabbi Amram Ben Diwan.

Eight days later, our group was to fly back to Paris. The president of the community committee learned that my exit permit had been stolen. He promised me that he would phone the authorities at the airport and arrange that I board the plane.

Our group reached the Casablanca airport by three different buses. Everyone was admitted on the plane but me. I remained alone and anxious at the airport, until a family member of one of the passengers came to fetch me and take me by car to the city of Casablanca. This was, I believe, my second punishment.

A respected Jew of Casablanca welcomed me into his home as a brother would have. He asked the community committee (of which a few members were friends of police officers) to intervene and find a solution to my predicament.

Three days later, one of the community members succeeded in obtaining my access to a plane. With a four-day delay, I was permitted to board a plane, as a lone Israeli. The committee president asked David Maman, the committee secretary, to drive me to the airport. I took my two suitcases out of his trunk and lifted the bag in which I had put the stone. I gave my luggage to customs control. Without opening my suitcases, the customs officers made a mark on them. They then told me to put my bag together with the suitcases. I had requested money for expenses from Hacham Meir Attia, who lent me all the money I needed.

The committee secretary and my host had come with me to the airport, as well as the assistant of the Jew who had seen to it that police and customs authorities would not bother me. They all stayed there until they saw me climb into the van that took the passengers to the plane to Paris. They did not leave the premises before the van sped away, and they bid me good-bye with hand gestures.

We stopped in front of the plane and boarded it. Relieved, I threw myself on my seat. Just before the departure, a customs officer came in and shouted, "Who is Moshe Dahan?" Shaking, I answered that it was me, and he asked me in French to follow him.

As we were going down the stairs, he explained that they had found a bag put aside, which they realized was mine. Inside they had found a black stone. They wanted me to come and explain myself at the customs office.

All this happened while the plane motor had started running and the aircraft was ready for takeoff. I was trembling. Here, they could hold me and arrest me because of a suspicious item! This was my third punishment.

Oh my! What did I do?! Why did I take this stone from the pile on the grave?! I thought.

The customs officer ordered me to explain the contents of the bag, the presence of the black stone. Would it explode during the flight? I explained where it had come from and the reason I took it with me.

"I know that you Israelis won't make trouble. But why should I believe you when you say that the stone is holy? And anyway, it's not right to take a stone from the sage Lachzan ben Amran's grave."

Fortunately, the customs officers accepted my explanation, for the Tzaddik's name is known to the authorities, the police, and the customs officers. They told me to close my bag immediately and run to the plane before takeoff. In a few minutes, I covered the distance between the customs office and the plane. The minute I boarded the plane, it took off.

Before I left Casablanca, I had told my family in Israel that my passport had been stolen. My son Amram had phoned his friend Mr. Moshe Golan (Gozlan) in France and asked him to have the Israeli Embassy intervene to enable me to leave Morocco. Mr. Golan had connections in the Israeli Embassy in Paris. Thank G-d, I did not need his help and I arrived safe and sound at Charles de Gaulle Airport in Paris. My son's friend was waiting for me at the airport and took me to his apartment in his car.

In the evening, Mr. Golan wanted to celebrate my arrival with a drink and a good meal. He had put a few bottles in the fridge in advance. As we were talking, marveling at the happy ending of my mishap, we heard an explosion. The bottles had exploded in the fridge!

When we had brought my suitcases and my bag into Mr. Golan's apartment, I had not told him that I had taken a stone from the grave and that I thought I had received my well-deserved punishment with my three misfortunes.

"Such a thing never happened to me," Mr. Golan exclaimed.

Without telling a thing to my host, I was sure that the stone I had put in his apartment had caused the explosion.

My error had cost me money and stress, but not health, thank G-d.

It was a miracle that I was not detained in Morocco, as it had happened to others. It was also a miracle that the customs officers did not arrest me after they discovered the stone, and that the plane did not take off without me.

Nevertheless, I felt that the Tzaddik had not forgiven my offense. I thus decided that, with G-d's help, I would make another trip to Morocco to return the stone to its place. In the meantime, I deposited it in the synagogue bearing Rabbi Amram Ben Diwan's name in Kiryat Gat, in the good care of my friend Yitzhak ben Shushan.

The day we brought it to Kiryat Gat, the worshippers placed it in the holy ark with great veneration. They firmly opposed the idea to bring it back to the grave. They said that, on the contrary, it commemorated the Lag Ba'Omer pilgrimages. For the time being, the stone is kept in their synagogue as a memorial.[7]

The saints are great even after death!

---

7. On the radio, Mr. Zeev Revach described a similar case to which he was witness a few months ago when he came on a tour to visit to the grave of the Tzaddik in Ouazzane. After she finished praying, a woman from the group took a stone from the grave to place in her apartment. After she entered the bus, the driver tried to ignite the motor, without results. The driver and some technicians tried unsuccessfully to find the cause of the failure.

Mr. Revach, a believing man used to miracles performed by tzaddikim, understood that this was a supernatural phenomenon. He asked the passengers to examine themselves, to check whether one of them had acted against the Tzaddik's will. Suddenly, the woman stood up and said that, without thinking it was wrong, she had taken a stone from the grave to bring to Eretz Yisrael. Mr. Revach asked her to return the stone, and the woman left the bus immediately. The driver turned on the motor and the engine started as if nothing had happened. The driver and passengers were stunned. This event caused a great sanctification of the Divine Name.

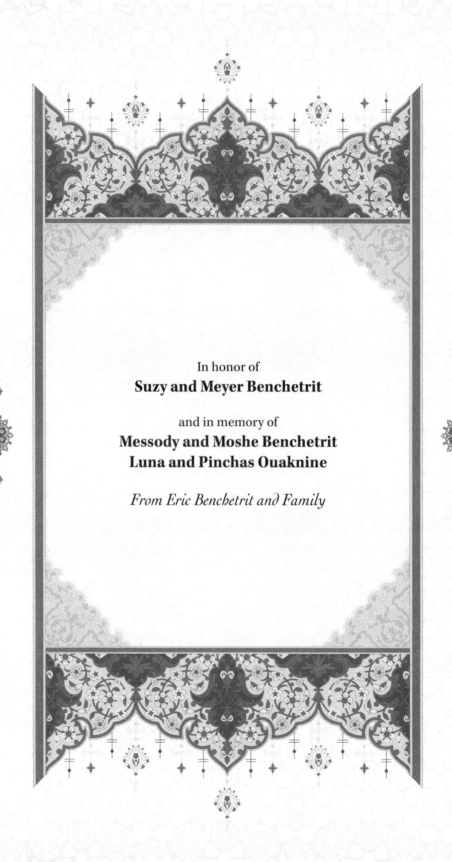

In honor of
Suzy and Meyer Benchetrit

and in memory of
Messody and Moshe Benchetrit
Luna and Pinchas Ouaknine

From Eric Benchetrit and Family

CHAPTER SIX

Wonders

Papa Patros Sees a Miracle[1]

MAN'S FAITH GIVES HIM LIFE, AS IT HAPPENED FOR A GREEK Catholic named Papa Patros. He worked as a waiter in a bar belonging to a Greek man named Santos. Papa Patros had so many Jewish friends who came to the bar that he too began to believe in Rabbi Amram Ben Diwan's miracles.

As the French officials were accustomed to do, the Jewish office employees also came to have a drink at noon or in the afternoon. Papa Patros, the waiter, was devoted to the bar owner. The boss totally trusted his waiter's honesty and gave him a free hand to run the business. He sometimes left the bar in his care for a few days or a few weeks.

When Lag Ba'Omer drew near, Papa Patros noticed that many

---

1. This story was told by Mr. Avraham Cohen, born in Ouazzane, who knew Mr. Papa Patros well.

The burial site of Rabbi David Hakohen at the right of the entrance of the cemetery of Asjen, 100 meters before the gravesite of Rabbi Amram Ben Diwan.

Jews registered at the travel agency for the pilgrimage to the grave of the tzaddik Rabbi Amram Ben Diwan. This pilgrimage took place three times a year: on Lag Ba'Omer, on 15 Av, and on Rosh Hodesh Elul. He asked his Jewish friends about it and they explained that the goal of this trip was to pray at the grave of a Jewish righteous man near the town of Ouazzane.

The pilgrims went to the *hillula* on the eve or on the day of Lag Ba'Omer and spent the night there. The next day they joined the festivities, the songs and the dances, and then went back to Casablanca to resume their work.

The waiter thought that the *hillula* was celebrated by a select few. He was surprised to hear that Jews came from all of Morocco, sometimes even from Algeria, and that the pilgrims numbered sometimes more than ten thousand people. The crowd was smaller at the *hillula* of Rosh Hodesh Elul.

The more Papa Patros heard about the pilgrimage, the more he inquired about every little detail. Where did the pilgrims lodge? Who took care of them? Who catered to their needs? The organizers explained every detail of the *hillula*, so that he knew everything.

One of the Jews finally offered him to accompany them to Asjen to witness the celebration in person. Convinced by the miracles, the Catholic waiter accepted to join the Jews who were frequent callers at his bar. He in turn told his boss Mr. Santos and his Greek compatriots the stories his customers had told him. When he asked for a two-day leave, Santos accepted, "on the condition that you pray for me too!"

Papa Patros left for Asjen, where he lodged with a family of *kohanim*. He was impressed by the "streets" of tents and by the "shopping quarter" inside the tents where food and drink, as well as lamps and candles, were sold. People bought boxes of candles by the weight and paid a porter to bring them straight to the fire. The flames went up to the top of the tree but the branches did not burn.

Since his hosts were *kohanim*, they were not permitted to go into the cemetery. They thus set up their tents outside the wall. They encouraged Papa Patros to go near the grave to see everything from close up and to pray for his close relatives. Papa Patros was amazed by the joyous atmosphere.

He recalled his boss's request and went close to the olive tree above the grave of the Tzaddik. He was looking cheerfully at the sight when one of his friends told him about a blind man who started seeing and a dumb woman encouraged to say, "*Viva Rabbi Amram.*" Men and women were enthusiastic, the flames licked the olive tree branches, and men walked on the hot stones.

He saw a paralytic whom people tried forcibly to put on his feet.

He was told that a man and his wife offered large trays of sweets and cakes, as well as a cup of strong drink, to everyone they met. This woman had been barren. She and her husband had vowed that if they had a child, they would come to the grave of the Tzaddik, distribute money to the poor and offer a meal and some sweets in honor of the Tzaddik. These stories kindled the interest of the Greek waiter.

He suddenly felt someone holding his shoulder and saying, "Pray! You should also ask for something from the righteous man of the Jews where he is, in Heaven!" He then remembered his promise to his boss and hesitated. What should he ask for?

"Some good health for me and my friend Santos. And also, that I should have my own bar and my own apartment. This will be enough for me."

Subsequently, he totally forgot that he made this request.

After midnight, he stared at the people singing, dancing and making *yuyus*. He remained so long on his feet that he was very tired and asked someone to show him the way to his hosts' tent.

As there was no light, he lost his way. Suddenly, an old man came in front of him and told him in Greek, "Since you believe in the Tzaddik, I'll show you where the tent you're looking for is."

When they arrived at the tent door, the man who had accompanied him disappeared. During the whole night, Papa Patros thought about what he had seen and heard. The next day, he related to his hosts what he saw at the cemetery, without mentioning the man who had brought him to the tent or the one who had encouraged him to make a request from the Tzaddik. It seemed to him something that everyone found natural and usual. He preferred to tell them about the hot stones, the men praying for the sick, the blind and the dumb, and the remarkable assistance extended to these handicapped people.

The following day, people began to prepare for the return trip to Casablanca that was planned for the afternoon. As a believing man, Papa Patros was deeply impressed by the celebration he saw. The trip to Casablanca took five hours, after which he was too tired to go back to work. His boss filled for him until the next day. The waiter then took back his job, both bewildered and happy.

As he was nearing the door of the bar, his boss Santos ran toward him, kissed him and asked, "So tell me! Relate everything!"

"What should I relate?" answered Papa Patros. "I saw people singing and dancing enthusiastically. They shouted '*Viva haTzaddik*' with joy and faith. What is unbelievable is that the fire rises to the top of the tree but doesn't burn the branches. I never saw such a thing. They did not even erect a monument on the saint's grave. I saw a mound of black stones burned by the candles they throw on them. Men run on these stones without their feet being scorched. As all the others did, I too prayed for myself and my family, for you and your family, for our health, a little happiness and a good life."

"Come here, my friend!" exclaimed the boss. "You can congratulate me! I see that your prayer was immediately answered! I've been told yesterday the good news that I received a huge inheritance from a family member of mine in Greece: houses, stores, land, buildings and money! Don't worry, my dear friend, as soon as the proceedings for the inheritance assignment are over, I will give you the bar. It will be yours! And my apartment too, I will give you as a gift to thank you for your loyalty and your behavior toward me. I'm rich today! This property is not worth a lot for me. You'll receive everything at no cost, for I intend to return to my country."

Papa Patros was convinced that his prayer had been answered.

Who knows? he thought. *Maybe Mr. Santos was touched that I prayed for him…*

He began thinking that the man who encouraged him to pray, and the one who showed him the tent at night, was none other than the Tzaddik himself who revealed himself in the form of a bystander.

For many years, Papa Patros visited Rabbi Amram Ben Diwan's grave twice a year and distributed money to the poor.

The Deputy's Daughter[2]

In 1935 or 1936, the daughter of a French member of parliament was the beneficiary of a miracle. He was the representative of the French citizens of Algeria at the time Algeria was a French colony.

A daughter of this deputy became schizophrenic. The deputy had friendly interactions with many honorable Jews in Algeria. The majority of Algerian Jews came from Morocco; they had told their children about the Tzaddik buried in Ouazzane and the

Aron kodesh of the Rabbi Amram synagogue in the *mellah*.

---

2. This story is well known in the Ouazzane community. Mr. Moshe Dahan recorded it as the community members recalled it.

miracles that would happen. Algerian Jews would come to pray at his grave with a deep faith that they could recover in the Tzaddik's merit. Because of these rumors, Algerian Jews recommended to the deputy to bring his daughter to the grave in Asjen—be it as a vacation.

The deputy concluded that he had nothing to lose and decided together with his wife to visit the Jewish tzaddik's grave. He asked the president of the Jewish community in Algiers to send a letter to the president of the Jewish community in Ouazzane, Mr. Eliyahu Amram Elhadad, asking to prepare an honorable reception for the member of parliament and his family.

Mr. Elhadad was delighted by the forthcoming visit. Together with the president of the *Hevra Kadisha*, he sent in advance a *minyan* of *Hevra Kadisha* members to the cemetery to organize prayers and readings of *Tehillim* so that when the deputy arrived, the *Hevra Kadisha* would already be present. For his lodgings, they prepared the house in which the president of the committee, Mr. Yosef Amram, lodged.

The guest and his wife were impressed by the welcome. They explained in French to their daughter that these men had come to pray for her. A *shohet* joined the group as well. As soon as they arrived at the cemetery, they slaughtered a lamb offered by Yosef Amram's father-in-law. The cooks who accompanied them began preparing drinks and food for the important guests. Every morning, the *shohet* slaughtered a lamb.

The deputy's daughter spent a few restless nights without sleep. The sick girl's father was convinced that the spiritual atmosphere and the prayers would bring about a change in her mental state. The Jews did not stop their prayers and the recitation of *Tehillim*. The numerous hours spent next to the grave were so exhausting that they sometimes fell asleep.

One night, the girl suddenly fell asleep at midnight. The following afternoon, she woke up calm, quiet, and clear headed. Everyone noticed the obvious change in her behavior.

Very moved, her father came next to her and began speaking with her. She told him that she saw in her dream an old man putting his two hands on her face and her mouth and telling her, "Stand up, my daughter! You are now sane and you have nothing anymore!"

Hearing these words, the deputy's face lit up. He joined the men who began singing songs about the Tzaddik, and drinks flowed freely.

The deputy immediately went to Ouazzane to announce his daughter's recovery to Mr. Elhadad. He asked him to invite the Jewish notables and the members of the community committee to the meal he would offer in honor of Rabbi Amram Ben Diwan, who prayed for her recovery. He promised to make known the Tzaddik's greatness and miracles.

That day, he brought with him a large quantity of drinks and a copious meal. All those who took part in it were very impressed by the miracle. The deputy distributed charity to the poor and offered a large sum to those who had come to pray. He was convinced that their prayers and the Tzaddik's merit were the source of his daughter's recovery.

A tzaddik is greater after his death than during his life!

The French Officer[3]

Between 1930 and 1931, a French officer settled in Ouazzane. The French colonial government encouraged many officers to move to

---

3. This story was told by Mr. Moshe Dahan. It took place around 1940, when he was still living in Morocco.

Morocco in order to develop the agriculture there, which was then still very primitive.

The French government gave credits or long-term loans to military officers, starting from the rank of lieutenant upward. Its goal was twofold: to increase the amount of agricultural products exported to France, and the loans encouraged the French officers to integrate into Arab society and find a source of living.

Free distribution of land was no problem, for Morocco is a huge country. However,

The great *posek* Rabbi Yosef Messas, chief rabbi of Haifa and all around.

the Jews were dismayed to see a French officer named Jean-Pierre Forniez coming to settle right next to the Jewish cemetery in Asjen. The land bestowed to him was on a hill directly above the site where many Jews came to participate in the *hillula* of Lag Ba'Omer, 15 Av, and Rosh Hodesh Elul.

In the beginning, the officer had various fruit trees planted on the land given to him for cattle raising. However, after settling securely, he began coveting the nearby lands belonging to the Jewish community.

The front part of the Jewish cemetery had been erected around 1730. In the beginning, this rocky land belonged to the Arab village of Asjen and was used as a passageway by the inhabitants. The surrounding lands were then offered up for sale to the Jewish community to enlarge the cemetery and to be available for its later expansion. This sale was finalized thanks to Moshe Levy, a wealthy man respected by the Arabs, who was the proprietor of a large farm. Thanks to his involvement, the Jewish community bought many hectares of orange and olive trees. This sale was finalized a few years before the arrival of the French settler Jean-Pierre Forniez.

The officer started disturbing the Jews and frightening the worshippers. This anti-Semite sometimes came close to the wall dividing the cemetery from the Arab lands and his farm. He started shooting in the air to scare the visitors, who fled on foot or on donkeys. His agricultural workers sometimes pestered Jews.

Seeing that his maneuvers did not succeed in driving out the Jews, Forniez turned to civil justice. At that time, rumor had it that the French had found a true paradise in Morocco. All the hobos living under bridges in France and the poor who came to Morocco at that time became rich. They turned into exporters and real estate agents. All real estate was in their hands, and, for all practical purposes, they governed the country. They thought everything was due to them and that they were the masters of the Moroccan government.

In the district and high courts sat French judges. There were also Muslim religious courts, but these did not judge criminal and monetary cases. Only French judges and certified lawyers ran the courts in Morocco. This is why Forniez was sure he would win if he lodged a complaint against the Jews and requested their lands located behind the cemetery grounds. He thought he could drive them out of that place, and the cemetery would remain an isolated island in the middle of his fields.

The trial lasted many years. The Jewish community hired the best Jewish lawyers. Eventually, thank G-d, the French officer lost the case. He had to pay compensation for his harmful intentions toward the community. He grudgingly had to be content with the lands granted to him when he had settled.

His wife was a nice person who apparently disapproved of her husband's dispute with the Jews. Years passed. In 1939, the Germans conquered Europe. After France declared war on Germany, the French officer was conscripted to the corps of engineers. He was sent to Lebanon, where the army had to fortify the roads and the bridges for fear of the 8th division, under the command of German Field Marshall Erwin Rommel, which had landed in Tripoli.

In Asjen, Mr. Forniez's farm began to feel the consequences of his absence and of the Arab workers' laziness. The war brought about wide-ranging poverty, so nobody bought the produce of his farm. Banks ceased giving loans. The German army overran the north of France, bringing about complete chaos.

Mrs. Forniez did not succeed in managing the farm, the orchards, and the property on her own, as the workers did not receive their salaries on time. She decided to entrust the farm to an Arab caretaker and left the village for France with her two sons. The French officer was shocked when he heard that his wife had abandoned their property and left Morocco. This blow threw him into such a deep depression that his military chiefs had to send him to a hospital in Beirut.

After the armistice, numerous French officers were sent home. Forniez left the hospital, but his mental health was still precarious. He went back to his farm and found it forsaken. He turned to Moshe Levy's son, Avraham Levy, and asked him if he was interested in buying Forniez's property, a proposal that was a 360-degree turnabout.

Avraham Levy went to consult his brother-in-law Yosef Amram, also a wealthy man. Seeing this change of situation, Yosef Amram led negotiations with Forniez. Eventually, Jean-Pierre Forniez sold his farm and his land for a cheap price.

The Ouazzane community saw in this ending a great miracle. The anti-Semitic officer who wanted to expel the Jews from their land around the cemetery with a lawsuit finally had to compensate them, and he lost his mind, as it says in *Tehillim* (7:8), *He digs a pit and makes it deeper, and he will fall in the deadly snare he made. His evil deed will come back on his head and his violent acts will tumble on his skull.*

May all our enemies be thus destroyed!

The Contractor's Fate[4]

Despite the recent French protectorate, Arab attackers and robbers would lie in wait to harass the Jews visiting the graves of their family members in the Asjen cemetery. The community heads therefore decided to erect a wall to prevent aggressors from sneaking into the cemetery grounds and assaulting the defenseless visitors.

In 1925, during the Rif tribes war, the president of the *Hevra Kadisha*, Yeshua Amram Bettan, asked to have this wall built immediately. After drawing the sketches, the president and his assistant asked a Spanish contractor named Candela to carry out the work. Candela began construction and employed Arab workers. Having heard about the miracles performed by Rabbi Amram, these workers were in awe of the tzaddik buried in the cemetery. It was well known that Arab women would come to his grave to ask him to pray that they be cured or have children.

In the course of their work, the builders noticed that Candela had tricked his employers by using cheap building material, affecting

---

4. This story was told by the president of the Ouazzane *Hevra Kadisha*, Mr. Yeshua Amram Bettan, and recorded by Mr. Moshe Dahan.

the quality of the work. Since the workers were dependent on Candela for their livelihood, they did not dare say a word to the president of the *Hevra Kadisha*. Candela kept up his dubious practices, mixing sand with lime—thus fashioning a poor-quality building material. To prepare the lime, he had set up a limekiln to burn the rocks at the foot of the wall.

One of the Arab workers let Candela know that the Jewish sage buried there would not forgive his dishonesty. But the non-Jewish contractor did not take this warning seriously. The workers were sure he would eventually suffer the consequences of his deeds.

Yeshua Amram Bettan trusted the contractor and expected the cemetery guard to keep an eye on the quality of the work. Once the western part of the wall was completed, Candela intended to begin the northern part. As the wall was very thick, he used to stand upon it to survey the work.

One day, Candela fell from the wall into the hot limekiln. The workers tried their best to take out his body, which was covered by blisters and burns. They placed him on a horse-drawn cart and took him straight to the hospital.

A short distance from the town of Ouazzane, they came upon Yeshua Amram Bettan, who was riding toward the cemetery to inspect the work. The workers told him about the terrible accident that had just occurred. They thought the contractor did not stand a chance to survive. The president of the *Hevra Kadisha* came close to the cart to see Candela, but the workers cried out, "Yeshua Amram! *Chalass!* That's it! Finished! Candela will not survive!" Yeshua Amram bent over the cart and saw Candela's scorched head under the blanket that covered him.

With his last strength, the contractor whispered, "I'm still alive. I know why this happened to me. It's because I tried to cheat you in the material and the work."

His head fell back on the cart. Candela breathed his last breath.

The faith of the Arab workers in the Tzaddik was vindicated. There was nothing left to do but bring Candela to the Christian cemetery in town.

To this day, the wall near the grave stands unfinished. Whoever visits the Asjen cemetery can see the incomplete wall.

"How wonderful are Your deeds, O G-d!"

The Attempt to Uproot the Tree[5]

When the sheriff[6] of Ouazzane ruled the district, he decided to uproot the olive tree near Rabbi Amram's grave. Early in the morning, he summoned two black men from his strongest servants, and ordered them to go to the cemetery, located five and a half miles away. With large axes they were to chop down the tree. The

---

5. This article was discovered by Mr. Moshe Dahan; it was written by Dr. Shuva, a military physician who, after his military service, became head doctor in the Ouazzane hospital. Aside from his job, he wrote articles on the town history.

6. The sheriff was the head of the *zawiya*, the school where the Koran was taught. The Muslims considered the sheriff a saintly man. The *zawiya*, serving as the burial place of all sheriffs, was a holy site for the Muslims. Pilgrims from throughout Morocco came there in throngs. The place was called *dar tzhemana*, "the house of the promise," for paradise was promised to those who visited it. The Moroccan kings, who were part of the Alawite dynasty, affirmed the superiority of the Sunnite dynasty of the Ouazzane sheriff. They disagreed on the subject of the superiority of their prophet's sect over that of Ali.

Before the French protectorate, the great sheriff of Ouazzane was the undisputed governor of the town and of the area, including the village of Asjen where the Jewish cemetery stood. Until they left for Eretz Yisrael, the Jews were buried in the Asjen cemetery. Throughout the generations, the anti-Semitic sheriff ordered cruel decrees against the Jews of Ouazzane. It happened that the grave of Rabbi Amram was vandalized. However, Arab men and women had been answered after praying at the grave to have children or to be cured. This had become common knowledge and had been detrimental to the sheriff's repute. This is the reason why he wanted to blot out all memory of the holy grave. The sheriffs always showed intolerance toward the Jews. With the arrival of the French government, their prestige slowly declined, until they secluded themselves in their *zawiya* and progressively lost their control. Being clever diplomats, the French showed them great deference but secretly limited from day to day their influence on the country.

sheriff ordered them to begin their work as soon as they arrived, finish at sunrise, and return immediately to Ouazzane.

The two servants had no choice but to obey. They placed their tools on a mule taken from the sheriff's stables and went on their way. When they arrived at the grave, they made sure the place was deserted.

The brawnier worker started knocking his axe on the tree trunk. He banged and banged, but his blows seemed to strike metal instead of wood. After an especially

Entrance door to the cemetery
next to the burial site.

powerful blow, the edge of the axe cut into the trunk. When the servant made a colossal effort to extricate the metal from the trunk, the axe flew backwards and split his head. He collapsed, wallowing in his blood.

Seeing his companion lifeless, the terror-stricken second servant fled. He returned to Ouazzane and told over the events to the sheriff, who could not believe his ears. After recovering from the shock of his servant's news, he ordered the servant to return to the cemetery with another worker.

The two servants removed the body from the cemetery and placed it on a mule; they left before the guard there could see what transpired. They feared that the attempt to uproot the tree would become known and the Jews would present the sheriff in a bad light. A few members of the Ouazzane Jewish community did become aware of the sheriff's plan, but to maintain good relations with him they decided to keep it a secret.

May all enemies of Israel thus disappear.

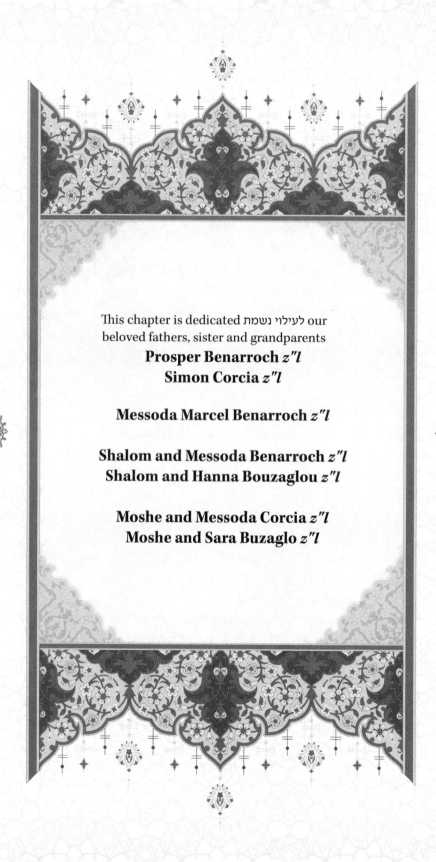

This chapter is dedicated לעילוי נשמת our
beloved fathers, sister and grandparents

Prosper Benarroch *z"l*
Simon Corcia *z"l*

Messoda Marcel Benarroch *z"l*

Shalom and Messoda Benarroch *z"l*
Shalom and Hanna Bouzaglou *z"l*

Moshe and Messoda Corcia *z"l*
Moshe and Sara Buzaglo *z"l*

CHAPTER SEVEN

Divine Intervention

The Girl from Casablanca[1]

A JEW FROM BENI-MELLAL NAMED YAMIN RELATED THE FOLLOWING story.

A religious Jewess named Lucienne lived in the Jewish quarter of Casablanca, close to a Catholic family whose only daughter had lost her mind. Madame Lucienne explained to her neighbors that the Lag Ba'Omer celebrations would soon be held near the grave of Rabbi Amram Ben Diwan. She told them about a few miracles that she herself had witnessed during her yearly visit to the Asjen cemetery, and suggested that they join her that year. It was in 1974.

The girl's condition worsened from day to day, yet her father did not want to admit her to a psychiatric hospital. Whenever Mrs. Lucienne visited them, she tried convincing them to join her at the grave by telling of the miracles she had witnessed during the

---

1. This story is related in *Ha'aratzat Hakedoshim*, and was recorded here by Mr. Moshe Dahan and the author.

People lighting candles on the grave of the Tzaddik. Everyone who goes there makes a promise of donation for their *refuah* (health). This photo is dated the night of the *hillula*, 15 Av 1996.

week-long stays of families who had brought their sick.

The parents rejected her suggestion. They thought that their daughter could not make the long journey and stay in the cemetery in such arduous conditions. Their Jewish neighbor was not fazed, and offered to look after the demented girl herself. In the end, the parents decided to make the trip with her.

As a high-ranking official, the father owned a new car. They rode to Asjen and settled in a tent provided to them in front of the Tzaddik's grave. A few days passed without any improvement in the sick girl's condition. On the contrary, she became even wilder. Some Jews looked after her and gave her sanctified water to wash her face with. This water had been placed between the stones of the grave for a whole day. From time to time, they surprised the girl by crying in unison, "*Viva* Rabbi Amram who performs miracles! No one can compare himself to you! In your merit, G-d cures those who trust in His help."

Most of the time, the girl's hands were tied to prevent her from harming those around her. One night, she had such a fit of hysteria that she tried to murder her parents; after her hands were untied, she leaped upon them, a knife in her hand.

The father stayed to watch the sick girl as her mother and their neighbor returned to the grave to cry and pray with all their hearts. Dejected, the parents prepared to leave after three days.

On the night preceding their return trip, the miracle occurred. At midnight, their daughter came back to her senses and calmed down. The bystanders were used to seeing her with her hands tied. How was it possible that she remained now sitting quietly? Her parents cried for joy and then asked her why she wanted to kill them. She answered that someone appeared to her in her dream every night to instruct her to kill her parents, and no one else.

Lucienne and the girl's parents were so grateful, their hearts overflowing with elation for the girl's recovery. To thank the Creator and the Tzaddik, they prepared a large meal accompanied by musicians and songs by the Tzaddik's grave; they invited numerous pilgrims to join them. In front of the Tzaddik's grave, the girl's parents made a vow to return and pray at his grave.

"The righteous will live by his faith."

The view of Ouazzane in 1925. The middle of it shows approximately the *mellah*.

The Skeptic[2]

A man recounted that he was an eyewitness to the following miracle. A mute was brought barefoot upon the stones heated by the fire which licked the summit of the centuries' old tree near the Tzaddik's grave. Due to the heat and the pain, the boy suddenly opened his mouth and stuttered, "*Ya Rabbi Amram Ben Diwan!*" Those who attended to the mute did not leave him and ordered him, "Cry out once more, 'Rabbi Amram!'" The boy repeated, each time more clearly, the name "Rabbi Amram." The people stopped pressuring him only after he pronounced the Tzaddik's name very distinctly. From then on, he started speaking easily in front of the crowd that encouraged him.

Upon hearing a friend relate this story, a visitor expressed his doubts. He thought the organizers had put on a show in order to trick the onlookers. One night, this skeptic, who was a teacher, saw in a dream one of his pupils whose father's name was Amram. The pupil said, "My father would like to see you."

The visitor recounted, "In my dream, I went to the father, who began scolding me and gave me a slap. 'Are you not ashamed to have doubts about what they say about me? You shame me in front of people!' I answered him, 'G-d forbid! I didn't shame you!' I then felt that I was being sent to prison. When I woke up, I understood immediately that the tzaddik Rabbi Amram was annoyed with me because I had doubted his power to perform miracles.

"I went back to sleep. This same pupil appeared in my dream and told me, 'My father would like to see you again.' As in my first dream, I followed the young man, shaking. I found his father

---

2. This story took place during Hol Hamoed Sukkot 5697 (1936) and is recounted by Mr. Ben Ami in the book *Ha'aratzat Hakedoshim*. The mute's sister told the author this story during his visit to the grave on 15 Av 5756 (1996). At that time, the mute was living in Kiryat Gat, Israel, and his speech was still slow, showing that he was once mute.

planting pumpkin seeds in his garden. He lifted his eyes and said, 'Calm down! This time, you don't have to fear anything. Nevertheless, from now on, be very careful with your words!'

"I woke up trembling and terror-stricken. From that day on, I began believing in the miracles and stories told about this holy man. I told people everything I had heard about Rabbi Amram, what had happened to me, and my dream. I never again doubted the miracles people told me. I regret that I had distanced myself from all those who heard and saw Rabbi Amram's wonders."

The Sorceress and the Guard[3]

The Arab caretaker watching the Tzaddik's grave was fully trusted by the community. For many years, Idris took care of the buildings, the storage areas, and the room in which the dead were prepared for burial. He had the keys to the synagogue bearing the Tzaddik's name. In fact, his role was to protect the lone men or widows who came to pray at the graves of their family members. If they stayed the night, he had to be on duty so nothing bad would happen to them. Once he saw that no Jew remained in the cemetery at night, he would leave the premises and go to sleep in his house in Asjen.

All the Jews from Ouazzane knew the caretaker and relied on his sense of responsibility. No meal was held there without Idris being invited.

He was also respected by the Arabs and the residents of his village. It was said that he also worked as a soldier who had fought alongside the French. He did not work as a caretaker in order to

---

3. The committee of the Jewish cemetery of Ouazzane heard the old guard recount this story. According to Arab folklore, a sorceress (asa'hara in Arabic) can effect a change in a person's knowledge, thoughts, and acts for a limited time. This story was written by Mr. Moshe Dahan, who heard it from the committee members.

get a salary from the Jewish community, he said, but out of a moral obligation toward the holy site. He was not a poor man; he owned land and herds of cows and sheep. Since his fathers had faithfully filled the same position before him, he felt he had a duty to follow their path.

The Asjen Arabs were anti-Semites and mistreated the Jews. A great number of them unfortunately became famous as professional thieves. Nevertheless, since Idris guarded the cemetery, the Arab villagers never tried to vandalize the place or harm the Jewish visitors. During the Lag Ba'Omer and Rosh Hodesh Elul *hillulot*, these villagers came to sell their wares at the cemetery. Some were water drawers and offered their services to rich Jews.

Even more than the Jews, Idris knew many true stories of the miracles he had witnessed on Rabbi Amram's grave. Some nights, he came from his village to make sure everything was in order.

One night, after making sure that no Jew remained in the cemetery, Idris went home. He went to sleep and saw in his dream the image of the holy *sied*, Rabbi Amram, as he had been described.

The Hacham said in the dream, "Idris! How could you go and leave me unattended?"

Seized by fear, the guard awoke and ran to the Jewish cemetery. When he came close to the grave of the Tzaddik, he was taken aback to see an Arab woman bent over the grave, digging the ground with her fingers.

"What are you doing?" asked Idris.

The woman jumped in fear.

"I dig the grave to take out a bone of the holy Jew."

The guard screamed at her and told her to stop. Seeing who was in front of her, she began quivering in fear and asked him to forgive her.

She said, "*Ya sidi!* I'm a sorceress. I came from far to take a bone of the Jewish *sied*. Thanks to this bone, I succeed in doing sorcery acts to make a living."

The faithful Idris arrested the woman and brought her to the judge. She was condemned to a few months in prison for desecration of the holy grave.

The Jews were amazed to hear that the Tzaddik appeared in a dream to the Arab caretaker. The community and the cemetery committee were impressed by Idris's merit. He arrived in time to prevent the scandalous act that the sorceress had planned to do.

Idris said that it was a great honor for him to guard the Jewish tzaddik. After his death, all the Jews who knew Idris remembered him favorably for his acts and his faithfulness to the Tzaddik. The community then appointed a G-d-fearing Jew named Shimon Sabbah to guard the grave. He did so devotedly until his death.

The Lag Ba'Omer Miracle[4]

This story took place before the era of the French protectorate in Morocco.

It was difficult to reach the Tzaddik's grave, and those who wanted to go there to pray had to ride a donkey or walk the great distance to the far-off village of Asjen, where the cemetery is located.

The sheriff couldn't understand how was it possible, on his own territory, that a righteous Jew performed miracles for those who came to pray at his grave, whereas he, the saintly Muslim, was unable to do so. In every generation, the sheriffs of Ouazzane, claiming to be descendants of their prophet, tried harming and demeaning the Jews of Ouazzane by imposing unfair and humiliating anti-Semitic decrees.

---

4. This story was told by Mr. Moshe Dahan.

One year, the sheriff decided to prevent any Lag Ba'Omer celebrations on the Tzaddik's grave; he gave the Jewish residents of Asjen strict orders prohibiting the celebration of the yearly *hillula*. He added that if a Jew tried to reach the cemetery, he would be shot without hesitation. All the Muslims faithful to the sheriff were to guard all the roads and paths that the pilgrims could take to the cemetery and force them to retrace their steps. A messenger warned the Jews intending to go to Rabbi Amram's grave on donkey or by foot to give up the pilgrimage, for the guards posted on the roads would shoot at them.

The Jews believed in G-d; they hoped that the sheriff would change his mind and allow them to go to the grave. One night, a miracle happened. In the middle of the night, the Arabs saw a huge fire rising near the Tzaddik's grave. Of course, the place was deserted and silent, for no pilgrims were there. Still, the guards saw the cemetery lit by many lamps and by a fire. They even heard the songs of the pilgrims. In shock, they ran to glimpse over the cemetery wall. They were taken aback to find neither burning lamps nor human presence on the premises.

They fled, panic-stricken by the darkness and the silence. The astounded guards returned to their posts without a word. Each one was afraid to tell the other what he had seen, lest he be considered a dreamer or a lunatic. The guards kept watching over the road, motionless, as the sheriff had ordered.

An hour later, the same sight appeared a second time! Again, the guards nervously went to check on the cemetery from the top of the rocks. Once more, the place was deserted, with neither sound nor light.

Instead of returning to their village, most of the terrified Muslim villagers scattered. Some ran to Ouazzane to inform the sheriff about what they had witnessed. The village chief and some guards appeared before the sheriff and recounted the phenomenon as well. The sheriff immediately understood that one of Rabbi Amram's miracles had occurred. To prevent the story from spreading among the Muslim believers, he strictly forbade the witnesses from telling a single word about what they had seen and heard.

After the fact, the sheriff obstinately refused to believe the miracle. He still hated the Jews and tried to erase all signs of the wonders performed by the Tzaddik. He immediately announced to all the Jews in town that they were allowed to go to the Tzaddik's grave and to begin the celebration as originally planned. He explained that he had canceled the *hillula* because he feared an attack by troublemakers.

The obvious miracles that had taken place near Rabbi Amram's tomb did not prevent the governor from carrying on his harassment and humiliation of the Jews; he ordered that the olive tree above the grave be pruned, and he forbade the Jews from sounding the shofar at the conclusion of Yom Kippur.

The Tzaddik Helps[5]

This story is about a Jewish woman who made *aliyah* and now lives in Netanya. Following a kindness Rabbi Amram Ben Diwan had once done for her, she made a vow to visit his grave and to host a meal there in honor of the Tzaddik.

One Lag Ba'Omer night before her *aliyah*, she visited the grave of the Tzaddik. It was raining very hard that year. The few Jews who were still living in Morocco and had planned to travel to the Tzaddik's grave had changed their plans. They feared that the unending rains would damage the roads and prevent them

---

5. This story was told by Mr. Moshe Dahan. A nonreligious tour guide enthusiastically relates this story every time he brings Jews to Rabbi Amram's grave, resulting in a great sanctification of G-d's Name.

Location of the house where the visitors used to stay.

from reaching the place in time for Lag Ba'Omer. Instead of the expected crowd, only a few Jews were present.

The woman planned to fulfill her vow to provide a meal at the grave during the daytime, but only six families were present. She was disappointed and upset that so few people would eat the meal she had prepared. Some advised her to take back all the food and offer it to one of the synagogues in her town (Casablanca, most likely). Everyone tried in their own way to reason with her and convince her. However, the woman had invested so much effort that it was impossible; she insisted on fulfilling her vow.

The pilgrims were still attempting to persuade her when they saw a bus full of tourists stop in front of the cemetery. They were Israeli tourists visiting Morocco. The joy of this woman and of the pilgrims was indescribable, and the Israeli tourists were more than delighted to be invited to the meal. In fact, that day they had been invited for lunch by one of the Jewish communities, but due to a delay they didn't arrive on time. The passengers had decided to make the best of their setback by visiting the grave of Rabbi Amram and buying something to eat nearby.

"The Tzaddik surely intervened to bring us here!" they called out.

They ate, drank, and danced, causing great pleasure to the meal's hostess. She saw that, in addition to the first miracle done for her some time ago in the Tzaddik's merit, a second wonder had just occurred—and the tourists left the place very impressed by what they had just experienced.[6]

The Angel Refael[7]

Many years had passed since Rabbi Refael Encaoua[8] married the daughter of the *gaon* Rabbi Yissachar Asaraf. Rabbi Refael was concerned that he had no sons, only daughters. He decided to pray at the grave of Rabbi Amram and ask him to intervene in Heaven on his behalf.

That year, his wife gave birth to a son, whom Rabbi Refael named Michael Yissachar, after his grandfather. Years later, this son inherited his father's position and became the chief rabbi of Morocco.

---

6. See a similar story in "The *Hillula* Meal."

7. Rabbi Aharon Monsonego, chief rabbi of Morocco, told this story in the name of Mr. Yosef Amram during the author's visit to the grave of Rabbi Amram Ben Diwan on 15 Av 5756 (1996).

8. Rabbi Refael Encaoua was born in 1848 in Sala, Morocco, called "the little Jerusalem." In 1915, he accepted the position of chief rabbi of Morocco and the head of the great *bet din* of Rabat, created after the French conquest. He soon became famous; his books and halachic rulings were admired by Jewish sages the world over. His exceptional qualities, his loftiness and righteousness made him a man of undisputed authority, in light of his vast knowledge in halachah and Talmud. The sages and the common people called him "the angel Refael." For more information on his life, see the introduction to his book *Chadad Vetima.*

When Rabbi Refael's family asked him why he had only one son, he answered, "It's my fault. Instead of imploring the Tzaddik to have a son, I should have asked for *sons*. After I made this mistake, there is no possible way to fix it."

The Six-Day War and the Victory[9]

On May 15, 1967, the Israeli army was mobilized after the Egyptians readied to attack Israel in the Sinai Peninsula. War seemed imminent. Soon, the Egyptians closed the Tiran fortresses. The atmosphere in Eretz Yisrael was very tense—a feeling shared by Jews the world over.

The warmhearted Jews of Morocco were worried about the fate of their brethren living in the Holy Land. During this disquieting period, Rabbi Aharon Monsonego decided to travel from Fez to Ouazzane to pray at the grave of Rabbi Amram Ben Diwan. On his way, he went to visit Mr. Yosef Amram, president of the committee of the holy site, and encouraged him to join him.

The rabbi's visit took Mr. Amram by surprise. How did Rabbi Monsonego have the audacity, despite the tense situation east of Morocco, to go to a remote cemetery in an Arab village whose residents were fanatic Muslims? Rabbi Monsonego was unfazed; on the contrary, he persuaded Mr. Amram to accompany him. Mr. Amram did not have the heart to turn his close friend down. He even brought along food and drink to eat by the Tzaddik's grave, as all pilgrims had done.

They arrived at the grave before sunset and fervently prayed

---

9. This story was heard during a visit to the grave of Rabbi Amram on the day of the *hillula*, 15 Av 5756 (1996), from Rabbi Aharon Monsonego. Rabbi Aharon lives in Casablanca. He is the son of Rabbi Yedidya Monsonego, who was until recently chief rabbi of Morocco. The Monsonego family is close to that of Mr. Yosef Amram, of blessed memory, who was the president of committee of the holy site for over sixty years.

Minhah, adding a *Mi Sheberach* for the Jewish people and particularly the Jews living in Eretz Yisrael. Rabbi Monsonego then turned to the Tzaddik's grave, crying, and asked him to give him a sign about future events: Would there be a war, and if so, what would be its end?

Following their prayers, at night, the two men sat down to eat near the grave. They suddenly heard the roar of a motorcycle. They panicked, but to their surprise, they soon saw a police officer before them! He inquired if everything was in order and if anyone had bothered them. He then asked Rabbi Monsonego for a cup of arak in honor of the Tzaddik. The rabbi willingly served the officer. The officer then lifted his cup and toasted, "Long live Israel! Long live Israel!"

The chair of Eliyahu Hanavi is still there today in Ouazzane, in the synagogue named after Rabbi Amram Ben Diwan, and people still perform *brit milot* there.

The two men had not even begun to drink when the police officer disappeared.

Used to witnessing the miracles performed by the Tzaddik, Mr. Amram was unfazed. "Here! By means of this police officer, Rabbi Amram gave us a clear and explicit answer about the future of the Jewish people!" he cried out.

The two men understood the message: The Jewish people would be victorious in a miraculous way.

Blessed is He Who sanctifies His Name in public.

To our dear parents
Shlomo and Hanna Torjmane
and
David and Lydia Rahel Wizman

Words cannot describe the admiration and dedication
they had for Rabbi Amram Ben Diwan. Every year, while
living in Morocco, they never missed an opportunity
to attend the *hillula* of the Tzaddik in Ouazanne.

You are an inspiration for all of us.
You constantly show us the right way
with your patience and love.

May Hashem only bless you with health,
happiness, and *berachah* in all that you do.

Simon and Deborah Torjmane

CHAPTER EIGHT

Marvels

Amram's House Is on Fire!

THE TALMUD (*KIDDUSHIN* 81A) TELLS THE STORY OF JEWISH GIRLS who were taken captive by non-Jews. The Sages ransomed them and brought them to Nehardea, where they were put up in the upper floor of Rabbi Amram Hasida's house. As those girls were particularly beautiful, the Sages removed the stairs leading to the upper floor so that no man could reach it.

When one of these girls passed the attic door, her beauty illuminated the house down to the lower floor. Lifting his eyes, Rabbi Amram Hasida saw the girl's dazzling beauty. Seized by an irresistible desire, he took a heavy ladder that ten men would have been unable to raise, inclined it toward the attic, and swiftly went up. As he reached the middle rungs, he returned to his senses and stopped climbing.

He started screaming, *"Nura bei Amram!* Amram's house is on fire!" His call alerted all the neighbors, who rushed to put out the fire. In fact, he shouted "Fire!" so that the presence of witnesses would stop him from giving in to the desire that took hold of him. He was alluding to the "fire" of the evil inclination that burned within him in order to avoid sinning. Among the neighbors who arrived were a few sages, stunned to see Rabbi Amram Hasida standing on the ladder leading to the attic.

"You shamed us!" they cried. "Everybody understands what you meant to do!"

"Better to be ashamed of Amram in this world than be ashamed of him in the World to Come!" the rabbi answered.

Rabbi Amram forced the evil inclination by an oath to leave him immediately. It left his body in the form of a pillar of fire.

"See!" said Rabbi Amram to his evil inclination. "You are fire and I am a being of flesh and blood. Nevertheless, I'm superior to you, for I defeated you!"

The synagogue Bet Israel in the name of the tzaddik Rabbi Amram Ben Diwan in Givat Olga. It was built in Israel, thanks to the efforts of Moshe Dahan (standing at the right). On the left is Avraham Cohen.

This teaches us how watchful we must be when walking in the street or in any public place—how important it is that our children wear decent clothing, fit for holy Jews.

We have quoted this Talmudic passage for several reasons. First, in all the writings of the *hachamim* of Morocco, Rabbi Amram Ben Diwan was affectionately called Rabbi Amram Hasida, after the Talmudic Sage whose above story is a teaching for all generations. Second, when Rabbi Amram Hasida said, "Amram's house is on fire!" he was referring to the fire of the evil inclination, which did not succeed in bringing him to sin. Before all of his neighbors, the Sage proved that a man of flesh and blood is capable of weakening the power of a raging fire. Finally, this story brings to mind the miracle of the fire burning on the grave of Rabbi Amram Ben Diwan without it scorching the branches of the olive tree.

The Olives on Rabbi Amram's Tree[1]

Whoever had an eye ailment and ate the small olives growing on the tree covering the Tzaddik's grave immediately recovered.

These olives constituted a drastic cure for eye diseases and trachoma. The Arabs who had tried this remedy stealthily went into the cemetery during olive season and plucked some olives, which they swallowed with water. They revealed this wonderful cure to the Jews. In fact, the Muslims used to make the pilgrimage to the grave of Rabbi Amram, whom they called Lachzan ben Amran, but not on the day of the *hillula*.

Now that the great majority of Jews had left the country and no one remained in Ouazzane, the Arabs guarded the grave with veneration. The municipality indeed took responsibility for caring

---

1. This article, a resume of the present activities on Rabbi Amram's grave, was written by Mr. Ben Ami and Mr. Moshe Dahan.

for the Jewish cemetery and the grave, and guarding the premises; no grave was ever vandalized.

A small number of Jews comes today to join the *hillula* on Lag Ba'Omer. The local and military authorities, with the Jewish committee's endorsement, keep organizing on Lag Ba'Omer night a military parade and a reception in the tent built for this purpose. This tradition had been established by the French authorities as a token of respect for the holy site.

Many Arab believers who did not live in Asjen came to the cemetery after having heard about the miracles performed there for the Jews.

In front of the trees, parallel to the Tzaddik's olive tree, the Arabs too asked "Lachzan ben Amran" to hear their prayers and cure them. Many Arab women had children after years of childlessness. Some families came from afar to lodge with their parents in the village in order to be close to the grave and to pray for their recovery or their deliverance.

Blessed be G-d Who saves!

A Snake on the Road[2]

Journalist Emmanuel Heyman described the olive tree whose branches growing over the Tzaddik's grave were never scorched by flames. As a reporter, he saw beautiful scenes which seemed strange to him, such as that of a woman who sat under the Tzaddik's tree for an entire day, inspired, watching the miracles performed before her eyes.

This woman related that another woman went into the cemetery during her period of impurity, although this should not be done.

---

2. Israeli reporter Emmanuel Heyman wrote this article following his visit to Rabbi Amram Ben Diwan's grave.

Inside the synagogue of Rabbi Amram Ben Diwan, in Ouazzane.

The woman suddenly saw at the entrance a snake raising its head and standing in her path. She immediately turned back, for she understood that she should not try to enter when she was not pure.

Emmanuel Heyman concluded that what he related was a thing of the past. The rooms that used to be occupied by the pilgrims are now empty. However, a man who had the custom to come every year and slaughter a lamb in honor of the Tzaddik did not abandon this tradition. The same year, 2006, he brought a large animal, which was slaughtered, cleaned, and koshered. After the meat was cooked, his family, friends, and bystanders were invited to partake of the meal.

After having drunk whiskey and arak, they began singing together joyously, accompanied by an oriental choir, "*Viva Rabbi Amram!* In your merit, our master Rabbi Amram, *namisi liviladina.*" Afterwards, since there were Israeli tourists present, they began singing Israeli songs.

The Child Named Amram[3]

Hacham Yehuda Elbaz from Sefrou knew well Rabbi Amram Ben Diwan, for the Tzaddik had lived with Hacham Elbaz while collecting donations for the Hevron yeshiva. Fourteen years after Rabbi Amram's passing, Hacham Elbaz's wife ceased bearing children. She asked her husband to pray that she would have another son. He then made a vow that if his wife would bear a son, he would give him the Tzaddik's name.

His prayer was soon answered: that same year, his wife bore a son. They named him Amram and this child grew in Torah and holiness until he was appointed *hacham* and *dayan* in Sefrou. At eighteen, he was already writing books and rendering halachic decisions.

An Eventful Trip[4]

In the spring of 1938, we traveled on pilgrimage every two months to the grave of the tzaddik Rabbi Amram. My friends and I—we were a group of seven bachelors—prepared food and drink beforehand and spent our visit learning *Tehillim*. In the afternoon, we prayed Minhah there and then packed everything we had brought and went home.

That day, our group was composed of Yosef ben David, Yaakov Elkayam, Shimon Dayan, Machluf Gozlan, Moshe Haim Elbaz, and me. We put our bags on a donkey, for there was no public transportation at the time. We went shopping for food together

---

3. This story is told in *Malchei Rabbanan*, p. 102, under the letter "Amram Elbaz." It is written there that when Rabbi Amram lived in the Elbazes' house, he prayed for his host's wife, and promised her she would have a son the next year and would name him Amram. However, this is not possible, for Rabbi Amram Ben Diwan died in 1782 and this child was born in 1799, seventeen years after his death. See note written by Rabbi David Ovadia in *Hakehillah Vehashadarim*, p. 176.

4. This first-hand account was related by Mr. Moshe Dahan.

before the trip. These supplies are called *frida* in Moroccan Arabic, and everyone gives a sum determined in advance.

We decided to walk to the cemetery. The journey took generally two hours, but since we were chatting and telling stories, it took more than that. Before sunset, Moshe did not feel well and decided to rest for a few minutes. Since he was leading the donkey loaded with the food, he suggested, "Keep going, my friends. I'll meet you later!"

We started walking more briskly, in order to arrive at the cemetery before night. Moshe soon lost sight of the group. He became afraid, so he called to us in a loud voice, and then shouted, but no one heard him.

Sitting on his donkey, he kept calling but received no response. He thought that robbers had attacked his friends and perhaps even killed them. His voice was creating a strong echo, and we had walked a fair distance away from him when we heard a powerful sound in the distance—it was Moshe! We imagined that these screams meant Moshe was being attacked by thieves. Panic-stricken, we started running toward the Asjen cemetery, unaware that Moshe was pursuing us on his donkey.

The five of us arrived breathless at the cemetery, convinced that our friend had been assaulted. The Jewish guard reassured us that Moshe would certainly arrive soon, but we were anxious. Our trip, planned as an opportunity to rejoice and to eat a good meal at the Tzaddik's grave, had turned into a nightmare.

Immersed in our gloomy thoughts, we suddenly saw Moshe arriving leisurely on his donkey. Our fears had misled us—each side worried about the safety of the other—but now the reunited group was ecstatic.

Thanking G-d that we were safe and sound, we fervently prayed Arvit and then read the *sefer Tehillim* under the olive tree growing near the grave. The next morning, we started praying without a *minyan*, until a number of Jews came unexpectedly and completed the *minyan*. We took out a *sefer Torah* and said the blessing *Hagomel* to thank G-d Who brought us safely to our destination. We all shook hands and exclaimed, "Blessed be G-d Who resuscitates the dead! We were saved from harm by the Tzaddik's merit!"

Take the First Step

There are many Jews who say, "If G-d would manifest miracles for us as He did for our ancestors, we also would believe in Him and serve Him"; "If we would see the wonders, we would believe in the Tzaddik's prayer"; "After being witnesses to the miracles and not only hearing stories, we would have faith."[5]

One must not think this way. Pharaoh and all the Egyptians witnessed a great number of miracles during the Ten Plagues and the Splitting of the Sea. Nevertheless, they did not hesitate to pursue the Children of Israel into the sea after it had opened.

The Children of Israel themselves saw the Divine Power, crossed the sea split into twelve paths, and saw with their own eyes the lifeless bodies of the Egyptians: *Israel saw the Egyptians dead on the shore.*[6] Rashi asks why the sea tossed out the Egyptians' corpses on the shore. The answer is so that the Children of Israel would not say, "Just as we leave the sea from this side, the Egyptians will also leave the water from another side and they will pursue us."

In *Tehillim* (105:7) it states, *They rebelled on the seashore, at the Red Sea.* Rabba bar Meri explains that this teaches us that the Children of Israel disobeyed Moshe at that moment and said, "Just as we leave the sea from one side, maybe the Egyptians are leaving the sea from another side and are going to exterminate us..." The Holy

---

5. See also *Neot Deshe*, p. 80.

6. *Shemot* 14:30.

One said to the angel of the sea, "Throw out the dead Egyptians on dry land." Hacham Huna says, "The Children of Israel in that generation did not have a firm faith."

If man does not want to see, understand, and draw the necessary conclusions; if he lets himself be swayed by his bodily desires, all the miracles in the world will be of no use to him. He has to make the first step toward faith in G-d and in the tzaddikim, and then he will merit seeing the rescue and the miracles performed either directly by G-d or by His pious ones.

Moshe Rabenu taught us this lesson even before he received the mission to redeem the Jewish people. Standing in front of the burning bush, he heard no word and no voice calling him. When did the word of G-d reach him? After he made the first step. An angel of G-d appeared to him in the heart of a fire, in the middle of a thorn bush. As he looked, he realized that the bush was on fire, but was not consumed. Moshe said, "I must go over there and investigate this wonderful phenomenon. Why doesn't the bush burn?" When G-d saw that he was going to investigate, He called to him from the middle of the bush. "Moshe, Moshe!" He said. "Here I am," he replied.[7]

It was only when Moshe went to investigate that he received the Divine call.

The upright men, who love tzaddikim and visit their graves, have perceived that the miracles occurred there in the merit of the righteous. They yearned to see and to know, and because they made the first step, they merited witnessing wonders.

A tzaddik stands close to G-d. He is similar to a servant who enters the king's palace without asking for permission. This is why we ask a tzaddik to plead for us before the Creator.

---

7. Ibid. 3:2–3.

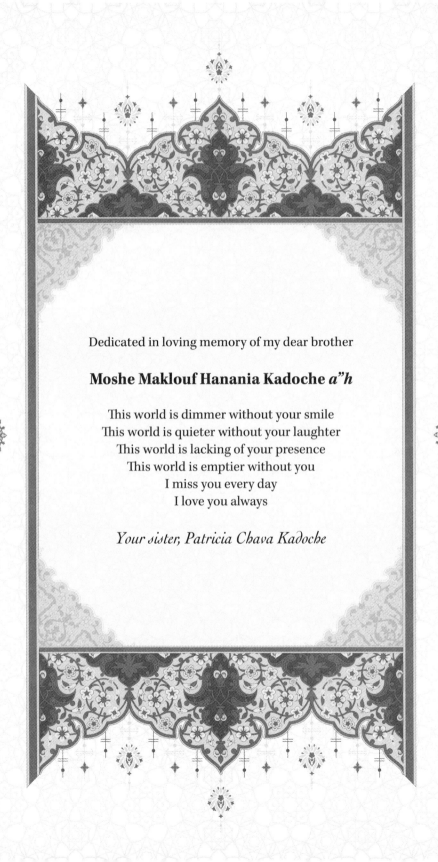

Dedicated in loving memory of my dear brother

Moshe Maklouf Hanania Kadoche *a"h*

This world is dimmer without your smile
This world is quieter without your laughter
This world is lacking of your presence
This world is emptier without you
I miss you every day
I love you always

Your sister, Patricia Chava Kadoche

CHAPTER NINE

Ouazzane

The Jewish Community of Ouazzane[1]

THE OUAZZANE COMMUNITY WAS BORN IN THE VILLAGE OF ASJEN. Today, one can still see in the village streets remnants of a Jewish community, such as the red and blue colors of the Jewish houses.

The Jews fled the village at an unknown date due to wars between Arab tribes. They settled in Ouazzane, where the powerful sheriff could protect them. The title of sheriff was transmitted from father to son, and the sheriffs' attitude toward Jews varied.

One sheriff had appointed a Jew named David Azoulay to supervise his house and all his wealth. His superintendent's influence was so great that if a man who was condemned to prison, flogging, or even death escaped and knocked on David Azoulay's

---

1. This article was written by Hacham Shalom Israel, *hazan*, singer, *shohet*, and teacher in Ouazzane, then secretary of the Casablanca *bet din* and assistant of Rabbi Shalom Messas. Today he lives in Jerusalem, where he is *hazan* and teacher at the Bet Shemuel synagogue. May he pursue his holy task in good health for many years to come.

The cemetery where Rabbi Amram Ben Diwan is buried.
From left to right: the Arab guardian Lachsen and Yitzhak Cohen.

door, he was set free because he had found refuge by the sheriff's protégé.

The tribes that settled around the village of Shefshawen—the members of Mashtara, Mazgalda, Rehuna, and more—did not accept the sheriff's authority and regularly attacked the town. The members of Mashtara once asked the Ouazzane Arabs to give them the *mellah* and all its Jews. The Arab residents' refusal triggered violent fights between them.

To be safe from tribal attacks, all the Jews took shelter in the sheriff's property, but my grandfather Yosef Amram, a child in those years, was once forgotten at home. He woke up and climbed to the roof. He saw the Arabs fighting and witnessed the flight of the Mashtara members. When he grew up, he made a yearly feast called "Purim of the Mashtara Members." I remember a phrase of the song that was sung during that celebration, "It was on the twenty-ninth of Shevat in Ouazzane, in the year 5652 of the Creation (1893)."

Here is another song in Arabic:

Kalu nezivu ala legras,
nidkelu lemedina balkias,
hel Ouazzane drabuhus balkertas,
bnei Mashtara meshawu maktoyin aras.

One of the sheriffs was completely mad and persecuted the Jews so much that many families went to find refuge in the town of Leksar.

On Wednesdays and Thursdays, market days, the inhabitants from the surrounding villages all came to Ouazzane, guns in their hands. An insignificant argument, for an egg or an onion, would result in gunfire between the villagers. The victim's family then ran to exercise revenge, and the fight would end in a bloodbath. They would then announce, *"Ashuk naksar"* (The market is closed). All the merchants, especially Jews, would flee, leaving their goods, which the savages would ransack.

Despite this state of affairs, emissaries came to Ouazzane from Eretz Yisrael, the most famous being Rabbi Amram Ben Diwan and his son Rabbi Haim.

One could write a whole book on the customs of this community. I'll mention a few.

When a boy was born, they made eight days of *tachdid* until the *brit milah*. They closed the boy's room before night, ran a sword on the wall, and read *Tehillim*, as per the Moroccan custom. Outside the room, coals sprinkled with salt were burning to chase demons away. They hung up on the door the head of a cock, an outside leaf of lettuce, and biscuits so the demons would eat them and would not harm the newborn.

(When a girl was born, they did none of this. Perhaps demons are not interested in girls? The Ben Ish Hai cites the Hida, who writes in the name of Rabbi Haim Vital, that the reason everyone is happy when a boy is born and sad when a girl is born, is that a girl had more of the primeval impurity than a boy. I thus think that the Side of Evil seeks more to harm the pure element which is in a boy.)

Bar mitzvahs were celebrated as they are everywhere, with one exception: They made a *hinah* (henna celebration) to the boy on the eve of the day he was called to the Torah.

The festivities around a wedding took two weeks: one week for the bride and one week for the groom. On Shabbat, they would bring the groom to the bride's house for a special ceremony. People stood in the courtyard and the women would sing *arovi*, a song lauding the bride's beauty and the groom's intelligence. These songs would insinuate piques by which each family would tease the other.

Often, the father or the uncle would think the offending words were directed at him. He would react by shouting or getting angry, and would leave the place in a fury. The participants would then fetch him and bring him back. Once he returned, the woman who had said the *arovi* would swear by the name of Rabbi Amram and of all the tzaddikim that her words were not directed at him. But to show that she was not defeated or that she did not fear him, she would add, *"Ana ma kolit, wila kolit uvaki nakul"* (I did not say that, but if you say that I said it, I said it and I'll say it again). Then the bystanders would intervene and everything would clear up.

We could write long pages about the *Hevra Kadisha*. Groups of people washed the dead. It was a privilege to be chosen to serve in the *Hevra Kadisha*. Having the list of all the Jewish residents, the president would draw lots to choose sixteen men to carry the dead body to the Asjen cemetery.

Before the French came to Ouazzane, the region belonged to the rebels and not to the governor. The last fighters for the French conquest hid in that region. Abed Lakri, their chief, had established his general quarters in Asjen. The authorities advised Jews that, for the time being, they should bury their dead in Beldir, a land they gave the Jews. The Jews buried there an old woman, but her grave disappeared. Since then, despite the danger, they resumed burying their dead in Asjen. Thank G-d, no unpleasant incident occurred during the burials.

When it rained—and it rained a lot—the streams and the watercourses would overflow and the roads became covered with mud. Regardless of the weather, the man chosen by the *Hevra Kadisha* did not hesitate to walk the six miles to the cemetery. If a man designated by lot was sick or out of town, they would enlist a young man, who would be paid afterwards by the man he replaced.

Certain days are imprinted in the memory of the residents, like the day Moshe Torjman's wife died. The inundations on the road notwithstanding, she was buried without postponement on the same day.

On the Mimunah, the day after Pesach, no man, young or old, went to sleep. Everyone (about 1,000 to 1,500 men) drank to intoxication. At five in the morning, they walked through the Arab quarter to the Agmir spring to wash their faces. The drunken men made a terrible racket; they then went to the pasha's house, where they rejoiced noisily. The Arabs welcomed the men warmly, for they thought it would bring them good luck; the pasha even gave them gifts.

There are many customs and beliefs that some naïve people

adopted. During the Mimunah, one man had the custom to boil an egg, remove the white, replace it with a hot pepper, and eat it.

Many other customs were adopted by simple and naïve Jews who lived in poverty, though happy and content. Above all, they served G-d and loved their fellowmen. One man would come to Yaakov Cohen on the Mimunah day to receive forty blows on his feet (the *tachmilah*[2]), and never missed it.

Another custom of Ouazzane Jews was to swear for every little thing in the name of Rabbi Amram Ben Diwan, for they had a strong connection with the Tzaddik and believed in him.[3]

The Arrival of Jews in Asjen[4]

The small Jewish community had settled in Asjen according to the absorption guidelines ordained by the great sheriff. This sheriff owned the huge agricultural triangle composed of the Masmoda

---

2. The *tachmilah* is a punitive measure taken by schoolteachers. If a pupil misbehaved in class, two children, among the strongest in class, would lift his feet. The teacher would insert his feet into the *flakka*, a thick wooden rod on which a rope was stretched from one side to the other. When one revolved the rope on itself, the child's two feet were caught, which allowed the teacher to easily flog the soles of his feet. A drawing depicting the *flakka* is in *Yahadut Morocco*, p. 170. See further the note in "The Talmud Torah of Ouazzane and the *Sefer Torah*."

3. The interdiction to swear in the name of G-d and in the name of a tzaddik, by Rabbi Yosef Messas.

   In this town, I witnessed an appalling behavior: Men, women, and children were accustomed to swear all day long, for the smallest thing, in the name of G-d and in the name of the Tzaddik: "Allah and Rabbi Amram." I rebuked them for this, first pleasantly, then more firmly. I mentioned the following: "They say to the one who is about to swear, *Know that the world trembles…*" (*Shevuot* 39); *A man deposited a golden dinar by a widow during a drought year* (*Gittin* 35); *King Yanai had a thousand towns on Har Hamelech and all were destroyed because of useless oaths* (*Midrash Eichah*); *Whoever associates the Divine Name to something else is thrown from the world* (*Sanhedrin* 63 and *Tosafot*); the words of Rabbi Elazar ben Azariah on the verse "Do not utter the Name of G-d in vain"; as well as other words that G-d allowed me to say.

4. This story was written by Mr. Moshe Dahan.

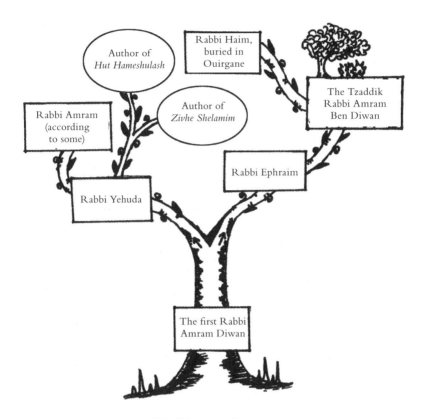

The Diwan family tree.

tribe in the north, the Rehona tribe in the east, and the Mazgalda and Mastera tribes in the south. Before the French protectorate began, all the inhabitants of the triangle belonging to the sheriff were considered his farmers and gave him a third of their produce. In addition to their agricultural land, the farmers raised cattle and beasts of burden.

Around 250 years ago, the sheriffs began calling various Jewish artisans to practice their trade and cater to the needs of Asjen's residents. In order that they not live among the Muslims, the sheriffs preferred to allow them to settle in the village of Asjen, which was a town deemed holy to Islam. Jews from Fez, Meknes, Rabat, and Marrakesh came to settle there. The city of Casablanca did not exist yet. It was just a small white house belonging to Spanish fishermen who came to catch fish on the Atlantic coast of Morocco.

Over the course of years, the Jews settled steadfastly in Asjen and became subjects of the sheriff. Some newspapers estimate their numbers at thirty families. Because of the stable economic situation of these artisans, Rabbi Amram Ben Diwan visited Asjen during his collection drive on behalf of the yeshivot of Hevron.

As Rabbi Yosef Messas writes in his book *Otzar Hamichtavim*, the Tzaddik contracted tuberculosis upon his arrival in Asjen and passed away soon after. As mentioned earlier, the local *Hevra Kadisha* attended to his funeral on 9 Av. When the news became known in the cities of Morocco, eulogies were said everywhere. Since then, Jews from all over Morocco come to commemorate his *hillula*. The first ones to make the pilgrimage were the *hachamim* and the liturgical singers of Meknes. They knew of Rabbi Amram's greatness and holiness because after fleeing Hevron with his son, he had stayed in Meknes for eight years. Afterwards, Jews from Fez and Sefrou traveled to his grave.

Each year, a great crowd came to pray near his tomb on the date of his *hillula*, together with the Asjen Jews, who for the most part were natives of Meknes. When the *hillula* day was well known, a large number of pilgrims came from all the communities of Morocco to prostrate themselves at the holy grave.

All of the Moroccan communities began celebrating the *hillula* day, with the sheriff's consent, only thirty years after the small community of Asjen settled in Ouazzane. As soon as the Jews left Asjen, the Arabs began destroying the houses of the Jewish quarter there. Until the Jews' departure to Eretz Yisrael, inhabitants of

Ouazzane visited Asjen out of curiosity to draw pure water from the spring used in the Jewish quarter. Among the ruins, one can see the walls of the houses painted in the colors used by Jews.

Some families of Ouazzane, whose fathers came from Asjen, continue to celebrate the *hillula* of Rabbi Amram on 15 Av, notably Moshe Levi, Yosef Amram, Yitzhak Seruya, and Machluf Seruya. At that time, the head of the Jewish community was a respectable man named Daniel Azoulay. The synagogue there was named after him.

Today, some families also celebrate the *hillula* on Rosh Hodesh Elul—the month of repentance.

Disgrace[5]

The humiliations endured by Ouazzane Jews, a minority scoffed at and denied its rights during the rule of Muslim leaders, were unbearable.

The harassments were dictated by the Letter of Omar, a decree prejudicial to minorities. It was also called the Decree of Dhimmi, according to which Muslims were to disgrace Jews and their religion.

One of the notorious humiliations was prohibiting Jews to wear new shoes in the street, unless they dyed them black. They were forbidden from wearing shoes near a mosque, wearing decent clothes,[6] and riding horses (they could only ride donkeys). If a Muslim came across a Jew in the street, the Jew had to step aside. According to the Muslim faith, touching a Jew renders a Muslim impure. The Jews were not allowed to have processions.

---

5. This was written by Rabbi Meir Elazar Attia, based on his research.

6. For instance, a Jew was not permitted to wear a quality *djellaba* nor a red tarbush (only black).

The Muslims were permitted to disturb Jewish funerals. It was prohibited for a Jew to raise a hand or to use physical strength against an Arab.

Moreover, the superiority of the Shurfa, the Sunnites' dynasty, a more fanatical sect, allowed adding other provocations against Jews.[7] When an Arab saw a Jew on the street and wanted to humiliate him because, according to them, he was cursed, he shouted, "*Haj!* Raise!" This meant, "Raise your shoulder as a sign of subservience." The Jew had to obey and make the gesture of raising one shoulder and lowering the other. Unfortunately, the Jews were used to this and understood the Muslims' intention. This happened before the French protectorate and only in the quarters inhabited by Arab villagers. If an Arab wanted to demean a Jew, he would order him to make the gesture of plucking out lice from his head. The Jew was forced to obey and make this humiliating motion.

Among other laws, Jews were forbidden to sound the shofar at the conclusion of Yom Kippur. I searched for the reason for this decree and arrived at the following assumption: The month of Ramadan does not always occur at the same time each year; it can fall in January or in October. Once in twelve years, the Ramadan can occur during the Hebrew month of Tishre. This means that our Yom Kippur is on the ninth or tenth day of the Ramadan. During those years, since Muslims fast every day during the Ramadan, Yom Kippur is a fast day for Jews as well as for Muslims.

At the conclusion of the fast, Muslims sound a long trumpet in a few places in town so the people can break their fast. During the *Ne'ilah* prayer at the end of Yom Kippur, we sound the shofar. So

---

7. These decrees were in force only during times of persecution and not in every town, until the arrival of the French government in Morocco in 1907.

that the sound of the shofar would not disturb the Muslims, their religious leaders made a decree forbidding Jews from sounding it at the end of Yom Kippur. This prohibition was not in force for the two days of Rosh Hashanah, however, since we sound the shofar in the morning, and not at night, therefore not disturbing the trumpet blast of the Muslims.

The Jews in Ouazzane obeyed this decree even under the French protectorate. They did sound the shofar, but said the words "*Vaya'avor Hashem al panav*" in a very loud voice to drown out its sound. A long time ago, the Jews in Ouazzane would bend their heads under the benches in the synagogue and the *hazan* would drop his head under the *bimah* to sound the shofar. Over time, these Jews forgot the reason for this and continued sounding the shofar in this way.

The *Talmud Torah*[8]

In 1928, an elderly man named David ben Yiflah lived in the town of Ksar el Kebir, in Spanish Morocco. He was a widower and did not have any children. He was a pious man, poor and very frail. In his youth, he was a porter; he was once robust and could lift heavy loads on his shoulders. Every day, he would wake up early to pray with a *minyan*. He often went to Ouazzane, which was a kind of twin town of Ksar el Kebir.

As a token of admiration for Rabbi Amram Ben Diwan, David ben Yiflah decided to offer a *sefer Torah* to the synagogue bearing Rabbi Amram's name in the Ouazzane *mellah*. He had such belief and love for the Tzaddik that he asked the community leaders and

---

8. This article was written by Mr. Moshe Dahan, who was present when the pointer of the *sefer Torah* disappeared. He was an eyewitness to the entire event.

the head of the *Hevra Kadisha* to bury him as close as possible to the grave of Rabbi Amram Ben Diwan.

The residents of his town were surprised to hear that he wanted to buy a *sefer Torah* for Rabbi Amram, for in Ksar el Kebir was buried the great tzaddik Rabbi Yehuda Jabali. Why did he offer a *sefer Torah* for Rabbi Amram and not for the tzaddik buried in his town? "The righteous will live by his faith."[9] Since David ben Yiflah was an old and pious man, nobody interfered and he did as he pleased.

He began saving money until he achieved his goal. He saved the necessary sum to buy a beautiful *sefer Torah* written in Jerusalem, covered with a velvet mantle embroidered in gold, with two pomegranates of pure gold to cover the wooden handles, and a pointer (a small, elongated object in the shape of a hand, ending in a pointed finger, with which one follows the Torah reading) of twenty-two-karat gold.

Located inside the inn was the synagogue called David Hamelech. The *sefer Torah* remained there for seven days until it was brought to the synagogue of Rabbi Amram. Every night, they said a special Arvit prayer at the synagogue.

The day the *sefer Torah* was finally inaugurated in the synagogue of Rabbi Amram was a day of rejoicing. The procession of the *hachnasat sefer Torah* circled the entire *mellah*. The women played drums continuously. Famous singers came from Meknes for the event and large sums of money were offered during the celebration, toward the maintenance of the Tzaddik's grave.

The Jewish community of Ouazzane and a large number of guests from Ksar el Kebir joined the meal sponsored by David ben Yiflah and cooked by pious women from the community. Drinks

---

9. *Habakuk* 2:4.

flowed freely. Whoever came in, be it only to kiss the *sefer Torah*, received a cup of homemade arak. Many women donated silk, velvet clothes of various colors, kerchiefs, and belts.

Once the *sefer Torah* was inside the synagogue's holy ark, David ben Yiflah considered it as having accomplished his life's goal. He left Ksar el Kebir to settle in Ouazzane, and every time they read from his *sefer Torah*, he felt immense fulfillment. This childless widower would be comforted of his solitude by his *sefer Torah*. His new community greatly respected him. Worthy families would fight for the honor to invite David ben Yiflah for meals so that he would not stay alone.

However, at that time, a very unpleasant mishap occurred. In 1928, the heads of the Jewish community in Ouazzane were worried about the children's education. As there were neither sages nor teachers in town, the religious education in Ouazzane was under the supervision of the *hachamim* of Meknes. Rabbi Yehoshua Berdugo and Rabbi Baruch Toledano sent two *hachamim* from Meknes, Rabbi Yaakov Berdugo and Rabbi Moshe Sebbag, to teach the children Torah.

These *hachamim* imposed a harsh ruling: Following classes at the Talmud Torah, children were not permitted to loiter in the street. If the supervisor found a child in the street, he immediately informed the *rav*, who gave the child *flakka* blows on his feet.[10] The education was strict and unyielding.

One day in 1929, the *shamash* of the Rabbi Amram synagogue,

---

10. The *flakka* was meant to immobilize one's feet. If a pupil did not know how to recite by heart a Psalm or a text in front of his teacher, the latter would strike him with the *tachmilah*. They would put his feet into the *flakka* and the teacher would strike him a few blows on the soles of his feet, accompanied by insults. The teacher would give the pupil thirteen blows, according to the number of words of the verse "*Vehu rahum*" (*Tehillim* 78:38). The other pupils shouted together one word of that verse, so that the cries and pleas of the poor beaten child were drowned by the roars of his friends. These were very

Machluf ben Shlush, discovered that the pointer of the *sefer Torah* had disappeared. The news spread throughout the community. Who could have done such an outrageous deed? Who dared take the pointer? Nobody could believe that such a thing could happen in Ouazzane, "the small Jerusalem."

Poor David ben Yiflah was severely affected by this theft. The upset community called the police. The head of the community committee, who was a friend of the police chief, asked him to conduct the investigation as discreetly and prudently as possible, because of the sensitivity of the affair.

We, who were children of eight or ten years at the time, could not believe our eyes when we saw two police officers in civil clothes going into the synagogue and opening the holy ark. We had known nothing about the robbery.

As children and pupils in the synagogue of Rabbi Amram Ben Diwan, we were shocked that someone could do such a thing and that the facts had been hidden from us. We were also distressed for David ben Yiflah, whose face was marked by sadness and worry. We were anxious to learn the truth.

Our curiosity grew from day to day. Then we heard that the son of an illustrious family of Meknes living in Ouazzane had yielded to temptation and, unknown to his parents, had stolen the golden pointer. This boy, having acted impulsively, put his family to shame.

The holy item was never returned. A few people offered David ben Yiflah donations to replace the pointer, but the old man made a courageous decision. He rolled up his sleeves and, despite his advanced age, went back to work as a porter to earn money to

---

distressing, unforgettable episodes. This punishment, called *atzla*, was carried out in most *talmud Torah* schools. (See *Yehudei Morocco* and *Hayehudim BeMorocco*.)

purchase a new one. The shop owners rewarded him conservatively until he had amassed the necessary sum.

The community members organized a feast in honor of the donor. They did it discreetly to avoid reawakening the sad affair which had caused so much distress. David ben Yiflah lived for a few years after that. Following his death, he was buried a few yards away from the Tzaddik's grave.

Before the last Jews left Morocco to settle in Eretz Yisrael, the community saw to it that the community's *sifre Torah* be sent, under the auspices of religious emissaries of the Jewish Agency, to the Israeli Ministry of Culture.

The Tongue Put Out the Flame[11]

The Jewish community of Ouazzane was very religious. At the time this story took place, in 1931, a few dozen G-d-fearing men habitually awoke at two o'clock in the morning to congregate in the synagogue bearing the name of Rabbi Amram. They would read *tikun hatzot, tikun Rahel,* and *tikun Leah* until six; then the other worshippers arrived for the Shaharit prayer.

Because of the piety and holiness of Rabbi Amram, the community preferred saying these *tikunim* in the synagogue bearing the name of the Tzaddik. Young men and children would join these worshippers in the hope of receiving a cup of coffee or tea that the *shamash* offered them as he offered the adults. Among these children was Shemuel ben Saadun. This is what he related:

One night, he mistakenly got up two hours before the regular time. Half-asleep, he went to the synagogue to join in the reading of the *tikunim*. As his father was often away on business, the child

---

11. This story was told by Shemuel ben Saadun, a reliable ten-year-old, to his school friends. Mr. Moshe Dahan was among them. Mr. Moshe Dahan heard this story from the child's family members.

went alone. He only had to cross the street to get to the synagogue, situated in front of his house, in an inn.

When he tried to enter the inn, he found it closed by a metal bar. He pushed the large door, went in, and walked toward the synagogue. The *shamash* who lived nearby had not locked the door with a key but only bolted it.

Shemuel pulled the bolt, opened the doors, and entered, waiting for the other worshippers to arrive. He was surprised to see that all the lamps kindled for the memory of tzaddikim were extinguished, except that of Rabbi Amram. Under the lamp of the Tzaddik, an old man was sitting and reading a book. Shemuel got scared. A few minutes later, he saw a long tongue leave the man's mouth and put out the flame of Rabbi Amram's lamp.

Shaking with fear, the boy looked for a way to run out of the synagogue and fled home. The sight he had seen so terrified him that he became ill. For three years, every little occurrence panicked him, to the point that his parents thought his days were numbered.

On that day, the worshippers came into the synagogue at the appointed time. When asked, they answered that the synagogue was closed by a metal bar and that they did not see inside anything out of the ordinary.

The town elders say that the synagogue named in memory of Rabbi Amram is sanctified twice—it bears the name of the Tzaddik, and when Rabbi Yaakov Abuhatzira came to Ouazzane to visit Rabbi Amram's grave, he lodged in a room of the inn in front of the synagogue.

Rabbi Amram's Belt[12]

The sultan, the king of Morocco, made a decree (*dahir*) saying

---

12. This story was told by Mr. Moshe Dahan.

that all the lands of the country that were part of inheritances or belonged to missing people were declared *vlad lemachzein*—belonging to the government. In addition, all the lands under the rule of the *zawiya* were granted to the sheriffs, among them the lands in Asjen. In Morocco, they called this authority *lachbush*. The supervision of these lands was taken from the *zawiya* heads. Later, it became under the supervision of the French government, which appointed an Arab at its head and granted him the title of *hanadr*. The sheriff of the Asjen region ordered the Jews to leave Asjen and move to Ouazzane.

One of the last families to leave Asjen took Rabbi Amram's large, colorful wool belt along with them. The rabbinic garb the great Sephardic *hachamim* of Morocco, Jerusalem, Hevron, Teveria, and Tzfat wore consisted of a long shirt, a coat, trousers, and a turban; a large, colorful wool belt was worn over the coat. (Muslim religious heads wore almost the same clothes as the Jews, except that the Jews wore a red tarbush surrounded by a black ribbon called a *tartur*.)

According to a newspaper article, thirty years elapsed between the death of Rabbi Amram and the transfer of the community to the Ouazzane *mellah*, on the sheriff's orders. A ninety-year-old woman brought along the Tzaddik's belt, which was then transmitted by inheritance from one family to another. At the woman's death at the age of ninety-two, she gave it to her daughter Aisah, who was married to a pious man named Moshe Parienti. This family kept a room in their house for the belt.

There was no maternity ward in Ouazzane. A woman due to give birth called one of the two old midwives of the town. The *segulah* of the rabbinic belt for women in labor was well known in Ouazzane. If a woman had a difficult labor, they took her to the room in the Parientis' house. Mrs. Aisah Parienti would envelop the woman's belly with the belt; the woman would immediately feel an improvement and her pains would subside. The birth then proceeded normally, thanks to this *segulah*.

Another belt belonged to eighty-year-old Machluf Seruya. He said that his grandfather Yosef Seruya, a resident of Asjen, had brought Rabbi Amram's belt to Ouazzane. It remained in his possession until his death.

As is known, *hachamim* had special clothes for Shabbat and holidays. This is why both the Parientis' and Seruyas' belts are both considered as having belonged to Rabbi Amram.

Rabbi David Hakohen of Asjen[13]

We know neither the country nor the town of birth of Rabbi David Hakohen. We did not find anyone from the past generation or any old men living today who could give us information about this *hacham* whose grave is on the south corner of the Asjen cemetery.

We were told that eighty or one hundred years ago, all the graves were marked by a stone of average size, sometimes by two small stones. At the time of our grandmothers, eighty or one hundred years ago, they started erecting *matzevot* of marble if the deceased or his family could afford it. The *Hevra Kadisha* members built the *matzevot* of most of the deceased in our generation. Before that,

---

13. This story was written by Mr. Moshe Dahan. I myself heard a few old men of Ouazzane living in Givat Olga, who said that this tzaddik belonged to the Cohen family from the Debdu village (see *Vayahel Shelomo* by Rabbi Shelomo Hakohen). I also saw that Rabbi Avraham Chamuy tells many stories about the town of Ouazzane, which he calls Wad-Jan, in his book *Abia Hidot*; among other things, he speaks about the sage buried at the entrance of the cemetery, named Rabbi Moshe Hakohen. On page 21, he gives many pieces of information and names of Ouazzane inhabitants. Rabbi Avraham Chamuy was a *hacham* and *shohet* in Ouazzane over 120 years ago.

they sufficed with a simple stone placed on the mound of earth after covering the body.

The Asjen cemetery was used by the community until the great immigration to Eretz Yisrael. In the beginning, only Jews from Asjen were buried there, but afterwards, Ouazzane Jews were also buried in this cemetery.

When one comes in through the door in the cemetery wall, one immediately finds on the right Rabbi David's grave, over which grow pomegranate trees and thorny bushes. All the small stones were put by people who came to pray there. Whoever came to pray on Rabbi Amram's grave would pass Rabbi David Hakohen's grave on his way and first kissed the bushes above this grave.

I am not sure if Rabbi David Hakohen was buried before or after Rabbi Amram. Mr. Yaakov Lasry writes in a few lines in his article that Rabbi David Hakohen was also sent to Morocco by the sages of Hevron. I presume that the void left by Rabbi Amram's death was filled by other *hachamim*, among them Rabbi David Hakohen. No one knows when or where he died. He is one of the holy men who are not famous, like Rabbi Eliyahu from Casablanca, for example, who is revered by the Jews of that town but whose family name nobody knows. The origin of many other tzaddikim, whose graves are disseminated in all of Morocco, is not remembered.

To my humble opinion, Rabbi David Hakohen must have been buried by Asjen Jews, as Rabbi Amram was. Perhaps he was buried far from Rabbi Amram's grave because that place was set aside for *kohanim*.

The pilgrimage would begin on Rabbi Amram's grave. I remember that as a child, we went to the graves of tzaddikim in Ouazzane on a donkey. Around 1929 or 1930, the Jews from surrounding towns began riding in vans for twenty people. In the end, during the years when many pilgrims came, there were several means of transportation and tens of thousands of people made the pilgrimage.

We, Ouazzane Jews, thought that one should go to Rabbi Amram's grave only on foot. Even after the expansion of the road, only a small number of pilgrims would use public transportation, for it was said that the Tzaddik would hear only those who made a great effort to come.

Before leaving the cemetery, every visitor felt he should also visit the grave of Rabbi David Hakohen. He was revered by the families of *kohanim* in Ouazzane.[14] Every year, they organized a *hillula* in his memory on Rosh Hodesh Elul, in a house, for *kohanim* are not allowed to enter a cemetery. Indeed, they celebrated his *hillula* with many guests and Ouazzane inhabitants.[15]

---

14. An emissary from Hevron named Rabbi David Hakohen was in charge of collecting the *tzedakah* boxes, which he called *Magen Avot* in the name of Rabbi Amram Ben Diwan. It is possible that it was the same Rabbi David Hakohen who is buried in Asjen.

15. To this day, the Cohen family from Ouazzane, who lives in Givat Olga (Israel), with Mr. Avraham Hakohen at its head, beautifully celebrates this *hillula* every year. According to tradition, the day of his *hillula* is 18 Elul.

The synagogue in the name of Rabbi Amram Ben Diwan,
located in the heart of the *mellah* in Ouazzane.

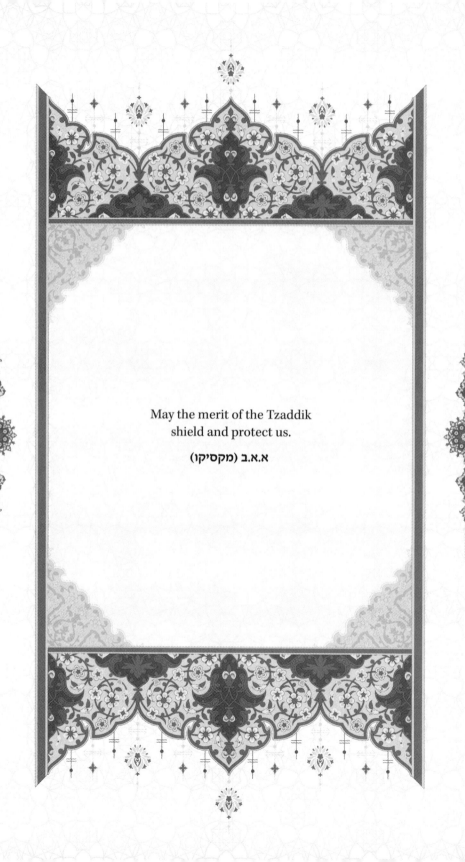

May the merit of the Tzaddik
shield and protect us.

א.א.ב (מקסיקו)

CHAPTER TEN

Collective Anecdotes of Rabbi Amram Ben Diwan

"A Prisoner Cannot Leave Prison..."

MANY PEOPLE ASK WHY RABBI AMRAM HAD TO GO INTO ME'ARAT Hamachpelah and ask our Patriarchs to intervene On High for his son's health. Was he himself not a tzaddik who had cured many sick people by his prayers? Did not people come from the world over to pray at his grave?

In the spiritual world, as in the material domain, a law exists: "A prisoner cannot come out of prison on his own." There must be someone to break his chains, set him free.

The Talmud relates a number of similar cases. *Berachot* (5b) recounts that when Rabbi Yohanan ben Nafcha was ill, his colleague Rabbi Hanina, one of the great *Amora'im*, came to visit him. As soon as Rabbi Yohanan stretched out his hand, Rabbi Hanina cured him. The Talmud asks why Rabbi Yohanan needed Rabbi Hanina; could he not recover without the other sage's help and prayer? Before this, the Talmud relates that Rabbi Yohanan had cured his disciple Rabbi Hiya bar Abba, so he must have had the spiritual power to cure a sick man. The answer: A prisoner cannot come out of prison on his own.

The Talmud also relates that when Avishai ben Tzeruya heard that Yishvi, Goliat's brother, had imprisoned King David in Nov, Avishai rushed to Nov to set him free. Seeing Avishai, Yishvi thought, *They are two men now. They can overpower me and kill me.* He threw David in the air and positioned his spear on the ground to impale him. Avishai ben Tzeruya immediately uttered a Divine Name, and David was suspended between heaven and earth.

Amazed by this great miracle, Avishai pronounced another Name and made him fall on the ground further away so the spear would not harm him. It is written, *Avishai son of Tzeruya helped him; he struck the Philistine and killed him* (*Shemuel II* 21:17). Rabbi Yehuda explains, in the name of Rav, that Avishai helped David by his prayer.

The Talmud asks: Did David need Avishai's prayer to be saved? King David was a tzaddik and could pray himself! The Talmud answers that "a prisoner cannot come out of prison on his own" and needs someone else to pull him out. This was the case for David.

We thus see that in every generation, even if tzaddikim themselves encounter misfortunes, they have an extraordinary spiritual power to pray for others.

Spiritual Entities Take a Material Form

The reader could ask how it is possible that objects come from spiritual domains, especially from Gan Eden. Our Sages say that in Gan Eden, the righteous are seated, their crowns on their heads, and enjoy the splendor of the Divine Presence.

Know that everything that exists in our material world exists in a spiritual form in the higher worlds. When the spiritual entity comes down in our world, it takes a material form. Here are the words of the *Zohar* (*Parashat Shemot* 13b) according to the translation of the *Sulam*.

"As the body is built in this world from the link of four elements—fire, air, water, and earth—and is formed by it in this world, the soul is fashioned in Gan Eden of four souls that exist in Gan Eden, and the soul is clothed in it by a body formed in this world... A man came up to Rabbi Eleazar and Rabbi Abba during their trip from Teveria to Tzipori. He recounted that he went into a cave in which he saw many trees giving out perfumes that he could not bear. There he saw a man, a scepter in his hand, who handed him sheets covered by commentaries on spiritual secrets and asked him to give them to Rabbi Eleazar. After Rabbi Eleazar read them, the sheets flew out of his hands."

This shows us that the secrets of the spiritual world exist in spiritual form which take a material form when they go down to this world. However, when they complete their service down here, they return to the spiritual world and fly away.

The Merit of the Righteous

Clinging to Tzaddikim[1]

After Moshe Rabenu split the sea for the Children of Israel, and following the many miracles that were performed for them, the Torah states, *And they believed in G-d and in Moshe His servant.*[2]

The Baal Shem Tov teaches that faith is the clinging of the human soul to G-d. How is it possible for man, a material being, to cling to G-d, an entirely spiritual Being? It is written in *Parashat*

---

1. *Teshuat Tzaddikim, Ma'alat Ha'emunah Batzaddikim.*

2. *Shemot* 14:31.

Re'eh that man is commanded to cling to G-d: *You will cling to Him.* How can he perform this commandment?

There is, of course, a way by which man can cling to his Maker. The verse says, *They believed in G-d and in Moshe His servant*[3]— because they believed in G-d, they clung to His servant. The author of *Tzofnat Pa'aneah* adds that when man clings to a Torah scholar on whom the Divine Presence rests, he really has clung to G-d.

The Midrash says, "If they believed in Moshe, all the more did they believe in G-d! Why does the verse point out 'in Moshe'? To teach that whoever believes in a Jewish shepherd [a spiritual guide] believes in He Who created the world by His utterance."[4]

Thus, if a man reveres the king's servant, it is a sign that he reveres the king all the more. G-d loves the person who loves and reveres tzaddikim. If someone belittles them, He upholds their honor even more than His own. When the idolatrous King Yeravam incited the Jewish people to idolatry and built idolatrous altars, G-d did not react to this lack of respect toward Him and did not punish him. But when Yeravam wanted to strike the prophet Ido, "his hand became paralyzed."[5]

It is even more important to cling to and to love deceased tzaddikim. For he who left this world as a tzaddik is a truly righteous man. King Solomon writes, *I praise the dead who are already dead [for they are rid of the evil inclination] more than the living [who may still experience its influence].*[6] Yohanan the *kohen gadol*, for

---

3. Ibid.

4. Ibid. 25:22.

5. *Melachim I* 13:4.

6. *Kohelet* 4:2.

example, became a Sadducee and a heretic at the end of his life, may G-d protect us.

Rabbi Hama bar Hanina says in Tractate *Hullin*, *Tzaddikim are even greater in death than during their life.*

May their merit protect us.

Faith in the Sages

Man must not rely on his intellect nor on his vision.[7] He should not expect to see manifest miracles and have his faith depend on them, though he is sometimes blind to this unbendable truth.

During his life, a person finds himself in all kinds of distressing situations and faces various trials. He must know that it is G-d's hand that guides the world, and that He gave His pious ones the power to change natural laws, as the Torah says, *The righteous decrees and G-d fulfills.* We must therefore believe in things that seem to contradict nature and reason.

The Talmud relates that Rabbi Yohanan explained in a lecture that in the future, G-d will bring precious stones the size of thirty *amot* by thirty *amot*. He will carve in them an opening of ten *amot* by twenty *amot* and will set these stones at the gates of Jerusalem. He construed this prophecy from the verse in *Yeshayahu* (54:12), *I shall make your windows of diamonds and your gates of precious stones.*

A disciple scoffed at Rabbi Yohanan's words: "Today we do not find many precious stones the size of an egg of a turtledove, the smallest of pigeons. How could we find stones as large as you say?"

One day, this disciple sailed on the sea and saw angels carving precious stones of thirty *amot* by thirty *amot*. "Whom are these stones for?" he asked them.

---

7. See *Sanhedrin* 100a. See also Rabbi David Shneor, *Neot Deshe, Parashat Devarim.*

"In the future, G-d will set them at the gates of Jerusalem," the angels replied.

After the disciple returned from his travels, he found Rabbi Yohanan expounding on another subject.

"Rabbi," he said. "Go on giving your lectures, for you are suited to do it. I indeed saw what you described."

Rabbi Yohanan scolded him. "Empty one! Had you not seen it, you would not have believed my words? If so, you scoff at the Sages' words!" He looked at the student angrily, turning him into a pile of bones.

This disciple merited seeing angels, something that few human beings are privileged to see. Nonetheless, he did not believe in miracles until he saw them with his own eyes—and was punished.

The Command to Fear and Love Torah Scholars

The Talmud (*Pesahim* 22b; see *Rashi*) relates that a sage named Shimon Ha'amsoni (or Nehemiah Ha'amsoni, according to some) explained that each time the word *et* is mentioned in the Torah, it implies an addition. For example, the Tenth Commandment instructs us to honor our parents, as it is written, *Kabed et avicha v'et imecha*—"Honor (*et*) your father and (*et*) your mother."[8] Grammatically, it is not necessary to add the word *et*. The Talmud explains that the word comes to add other people that one must honor; the first *et* includes the second wife of one's father and the second, the second husband of one's mother.

However, when he came to the verse, *Et Hashem Elokecha tira*— "Fear (*et*) the Almighty, your G-d," Shimon Ha'amsoni was ready to abandon his whole commentary, for the word *et* could not add anything in that verse. Can one add anyone to G-d?

---

8. *Shemot* 20:12.

Surprised by his decision to give up his interpretation, his disciples asked, "Rabbi! What will be with all the instances of the word *et* that you explained until now? You taught that the word comes to add something, and now you go back on your words?"

"The same way I received a reward for my commentary, I shall receive a reward for giving it up," Shimon Ha'amsoni replied. He thought it impossible to explain the word *et* as an addition in the above verse; therefore his approach to explaining all the other instances became irrelevant.

Rabbi Akiva, however, found the meaning of *et* here as an addition—*et* here refers to Torah scholars! The fear we have toward a scholar must be similar to that which we feel for G-d.

Some Sages asked themselves[9] why Shimon Ha'amsoni had not asked this same question when he explained the verse, *You will love (et) the Almighty, your G-d*, that appears earlier in the Torah in *Parashat Va'ethanan.*[10] Indeed, the verse, *Fear the Almighty, your G-d*, comes later, in *Parashat Ekev.*[11] Our Sages explain that when it is a question of love of G-d, it is easy to say that this love must include the scholars. But when the Torah speaks of fear of G-d—which implies reward and punishment—it is not so obvious to associate fear of scholars. Therefore Rabbi Akiva provided this explanation.

We see how important it is to love and fear the scholars, the sages of the Torah. Simple people perform this commandment with love, joy, and songs, as these stories of the rabbi show. G-d Himself loves His pious ones and executes their will, as it says, *He performs the will of those who fear Him.*[12] Even more, we, His servants,

---

9. *Pesahim* 22b, see *Iyunim* by Rabbi Ibn Israel.

10. *Devarim* 6:5.

11. Ibid. 10:20.

12. *Tehillim* 145:19.

must love His pious ones and endeavor to emulate their behavior, their piety, and their holiness. They will pray for us and plead on our behalf so that our requests be granted by G-d with mercy, and that the following verse be applied to us: *Even before they call, I shall answer them.*[13]

How much must they be praised!

Naming a Child after a Tzaddik

A man's name is connected to his mission in this world, as our Sages say. *Where is Esther alluded to in the Torah? In the verse "And I shall surely hide* (haster astir) *My face on that day."*[14] Esther's name symbolizes her mission to reveal the Divine Providence in every situation, even if the Providence is hidden.

The Midrash says[15] on the verse, *A name is better* (nivchar) *than great riches,*[16] that Moshe's name, as it is written—*If not for Moshe His chosen one* (vechiro, same root as *nivchar*),"[17] and *I [G-d] shall know you [Moshe] by your name*[18]—is better than Korah's riches—Korah paid for 250 fire pans.[19] G-d said to Korah, "You boast because you are rich? Moshe's name is better than all your riches!"

Numerous details of man's life are revealed in his name. The author of *Amude Shamayim* writes in the Arizal's name:

> Be it from the side of good or from the side of
> evil, in which way good or evil will be in him,

---

13. *Yeshayahu* 65:24.

14. *Hullin* 139b.

15. *Midrash Rabbah, parashah* 33.

16. *Mishle* 22:1.

17. *Tehillim* 106:23.

18. *Shemot* 33:17.

19. *Bamidbar* 16.

everything is seen by his name and everything is alluded to in his name. Not only the name, but even the numerical value of the name—every letter and every vowel—everything shows the deeds and the qualities of man. Everything in man, great or small, is alluded to in his name. If one sees a wicked man whose name evokes good, it shows that there is a spark of good within him. This is why the first sages who knew this secret would examine the names.[20]

Rabbi Meir Baal Haness would read people's names, as the Talmud says.[21] A number of *hachamim* stopped at an inn owned by a man named Kidor. Rabbi Meir said that this man was wicked, for his name is evoked in the verse, *They are a generation* (kidor) *which reverses itself, sons whom cannot be trusted.*[22] The other Sages did not reflect on his name and left their belongings at the inn, whereas Rabbi Meir took his with him. Eventually, the Sages' belongings were stolen.

Our master the Vilna Gaon knew where the Torah alluded to the name of every Jew. His own name, he said, was alluded to in the verse, *You must have a full, honest weight* (even shelemah).[23] The words *even shelemah* contains the initials of the name **E**liyahu **b**en **She**lomo (aleph, bet, shin). In the *Haftarah* of the same *parashah* (Ki Tetze), the Gaon saw his name and his mission in the verse, *I will gather you with great compassion.*[24] These words have a numerical value of 606, as does his name, Eliyahu ben Shelomo Zalman.

---

20. *Amude Shamayim*, letter 23.

21. *Yoma* 83b.

22. *Devarim* 32:20.

23. Ibid. 25:15.

24. *Yeshayahu* 54:7.

In *Sefer Hagilgulim* (ch. 59) the Arizal teaches that a man's name is the name written on the Divine Throne from where man's soul is taken. The name that parents give their child is written On High on the Throne of Glory, and this is how the child is called On High. Nothing is due to chance: G-d causes parents to choose a name for their child that way. This is why Rabbi Meir knew how to see in a man's name the number of parts of fire, air, water, and dust elements of which he was made.

This was the wisdom of Adam Harishon; he named each creature according to the proportion of the four elements it contained. Rabbenu Bechayeh says that Adam knew, by the wisdom of the letters in each name, how to name each creature according to its nature (e.g., its level of strength, agility, cruelty, etc.).

"Adam saw and knew the power of each soul, by which combination of letters it had been created, formed, and made, and from which letters emanated its life" (*Ateret Tzvi*, part I, quoting *Likute Or HaHaim*). "Our Sages told us that the soul's root comes from the letters of man's name" (*Bet Yisrael*). "The name of a man is the name of the soul. When man sins, his soul is damaged because evil attaches itself to it. This is why Rabbi Meir checked the names" (*Or HaHaim, Bamidbar* 25:14).

The name that parents give their child is thus the name of man's holy soul. Naming a child after a tzaddik influences his spiritual state. If the parents educate this child in the path of Torah and fear of Heaven, he will very easily acquire the tzaddik's Torah and holiness of soul.

The *Noam Elimelech* (*Bamidbar, Parashat Nasso*) writes, "G-d decreed in the creation of the world that there would be so many Reuvens and so many Shimons. If he gives the name of a tzaddik who has lived, this will cause a person to be a tzaddik, for the tzaddik's light in the Upper World is stirred up."

In the following example, we see that the Divine decree rests on man's name and influences the person bearing this name.

The *Midrash Aggadah* (quoted by Rashi on *Shemuel I* 1:23) recounts that a heavenly voice announced that a tzaddik by the name of Shemuel would soon be born. Many mothers named their newborn sons Shemuel, and all of them later became prophets. We infer from this that people bearing the same name come from the same root, which is linked to a heavenly sphere (*sefirah*).

We saw in a previous chapter that Rabbi Amram said to a family that had only daughters to name their newborn daughter Fadina, meaning "finished." This name affected the child's mother who, after that, had only boys.

We also saw (in "The Child Named Amram") that the Elbaz family from Sefrou named their son Amram after the Tzaddik. This child became a tzaddik, one of the great *poskim* of his generation. All the families of Ouazzane named a son after the Tzaddik buried among them, for his name brings them blessing and makes them become an *am ram* (lofty nation). Each of them bears this name with pride.

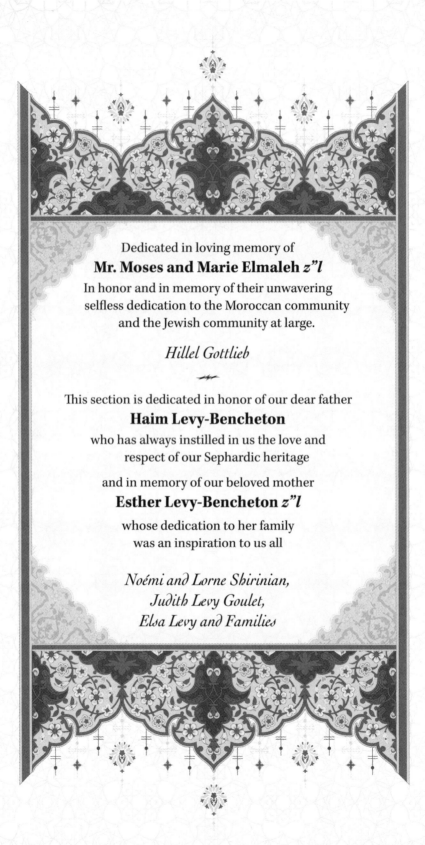

Dedicated in loving memory of
Mr. Moses and Marie Elmaleh *z"l*
In honor and in memory of their unwavering
selfless dedication to the Moroccan community
and the Jewish community at large.

Hillel Gottlieb

This section is dedicated in honor of our dear father
Haim Levy-Bencheton
who has always instilled in us the love and
respect of our Sephardic heritage

and in memory of our beloved mother
Esther Levy-Bencheton *z"l*

whose dedication to her family
was an inspiration to us all

Noémi and Lorne Shirinian,
Judith Levy Goulet,
Elsa Levy and Families

CHAPTER ELEVEN

The Graves of Tzaddikim

The Power of *Hachamim*

FOR HUNDREDS OF YEARS, PEOPLE HAVE VISITED THE GRAVES OF holy men; they pray there and request that the tzaddik intervene for them before the Creator. These tzaddikim gave their bodies and souls to learn Torah, rectified their character traits, and withdrew from worldly pleasures. Whereas some people despised their way of life during their lifetimes, calling them "primitive" after their deaths, all come to prostrate themselves on their graves and tremble when they hear their names.

In contrast, there are non-Jewish kings, princes, and officials who are forgotten a mere few years following their deaths. A small number of admirers mention their names from time to time, but they certainly do not visit their graves.

This proves where real greatness resides. We must be proud that these righteous men are the guides of the Jewish people, men of

Synagogue near the burial place of Rabbi Amram Ben Diwan in Ouazzane.

eternal greatness. Let us draw strength from their deeds during their lifetimes, and from their influence after their deaths.

Marking the Grave

It is an ancient custom to erect a *matzevah* on a gravesite—in particular those of tzaddikim. In Hebrew this is called a *tziyun* (mark), as a *matzevah* marks and identifies a grave. The Rambam defines this mitzvah in *Hilchot Avelut* (4:4), "One marks the whole cemetery and builds a *nefesh* on the grave." The author of *Yeffe To'ar* explains that this gives satisfaction to the dead because the mark is visible. "The memory of the righteous is a blessing"—thanks to the *matzevah*, we will forever mention the name of the dead for a blessing. Moreover, future generations will know his place of rest in order to pray there, ask for the tzaddik's forgiveness, and so on.

The Mishnah says that it is permitted to mark graves on Hol Hamoed to make them visible and to make known that *tumat met* (impurity caused by a dead person) is found there.[1] Graves were marked with white lime, evoking the white color of the bones buried there. Thus, people who ate *terumah* (*kohanim* and their families) refrained from walking through these places.

Rabbi Shimon ben Pazi asks where the Torah alludes to the fact that one must mark a grave. The Talmud answers with the verse in *Yehezkel*, *He saw a human bone and built a* tziyun. The Ritva emphasizes that the Sages thought that this mark—though necessary and useful—is mentioned in the Torah by allusion only.

We thus see two reasons for erecting a *matzevah*: it gives pleasure to the dead since he is mentioned in that place and his children pray there; and it makes known that bones are there, delineating the presence of *tumat met*. However, these two reasons do not apply to the grave of a tzaddik. The tzaddik does not need to be mentioned, for his words and deeds mention his name, as the Rambam writes, "One does not erect a *matzevah* on the graves of tzaddikim because their words are their remembrance." Revealing *tumat met* is irrelevant for a tzaddik since he does not generate impurity. The Mishnah (*Sotah* 49b) says that since Rabbi Gamliel the Elder's death, the honor of the Torah has disappeared, and purity and abstinence are dead. A tzaddik is pure and detached from things that bring man to impurity.

The *Zohar* (*Bereshit* 168a) states, "Rabbi Elazar says: Whoever learns Torah for its sake does not die by the hand of the evil inclination—the Angel of Death—because he firmly grasps the Tree of Life, which is the Torah. This is why the bodies of righteous men who learned Torah do not become impure following their deaths; the spirit of impurity does not rest on them."[2]

---

1. See first mishnah in *Moed Katan* and *Moed Katan* 5a, with Rashi. See *Pilpula Harifta*, p. 145.

2. See *Masoret HaZohar*. The Sages once saw the prophet Eliyahu walking between graves

The two reasons cited above thus do not apply to the tzaddik Rabbi Amram Ben Diwan since he did not leave behind family members who could be at his grave, except for his unmarried son Rabbi Haim. Tzaddikim do not require prayers for the elevation of their souls, as the Rambam teaches. The *Yerushalmi* also states, *Rabbi Shimon ben Gamliel says: One does not make a monument for tzaddikim, for their words are their remembrance.*[3] Furthermore, there is no impurity on the grave of a holy man, for the body of a tzaddik does not become impure after death.[4]

A question arises: How could Yaakov Avinu build a *matzevah* on Rahel Imenu's grave, as the verse says, *Yaakov erected a monument on her grave. It is the monument which is on Rahel's tomb until this day?*[5] We can find the answer in Rashi's commentary on the verse, *When I was coming from Padan, Rahel died on me. It was in Canaan, a short distance before we came to Efrat. I buried her there along the road to Efrat, which is Bet Lehem.*[6] When Yaakov said to Yosef, "I shall be buried there," he meant: "I know that you are upset with me because I did not carry [Rahel] to Bet Lehem to bring her to land.[7] I buried her on the road only [and not in a village]. However, know that I buried her there according to G-d's command so that she would

---

of righteous men. They asked him, "You are a *kohen*! How can you walk among graves of dead who convey impurity?" He answered, "The dead tzaddikim do not render one impure." See also *Zohar, Bereshit* 164a.

3. *Shekalim* 2:5.

4. This is not intended to decide practical halachah. According to some, a *kohen* should not approach the graves of righteous men.

5. *Bereshit* 35:20.

6. Ibid. 48:7.

7. See the Re'em's notes and *Leket Habahir* on Rashi. "Bring her to land" means: "to inhabited land" and not "to the Holy Land." It is clear that Rahel was buried in the land of Canaan, for it was there that she gave birth to Binyamin and passed away, as it says, *"Rahel died on me. It was in Canaan."*

help her descendants when Nevuzaradan would exile them." When they walked on this road, Rahel went out of her grave, and cried and prayed for them, as it is written, "A voice is heard On High... [Rahel cries for her children]" and G-d answered her, "Your deed is rewarded, says G-d."

Rashi teaches us that Yaakov erected a monument on his wife's grave for the benefit of the Jewish people who would come to pray there. The Midrash also says, "Why did Yaakov bury Rahel on the road to Efrat? Because he saw that the exiles would go past that place. He interred her there so she could pray for them" (*Midrash Rabbah* 82:11).

Nonetheless, some tzaddikim do not want a monument erected on their graves due to their humility, in particular righteous men like Rabbi Amram Ben Diwan, who, in his own lifetime, performed miracles and cured the sick through his blessings. He feared that after his death, simple people would worship him like an idol, especially if they saw a magnificent monument on his grave. Perhaps they might forget the most important thing—that a tzaddik prays to G-d and asks Him to answer his requests for those who prostrate themselves on his gravesite.

This is why Rabbi Amram asked the *Hevra Kadisha* to mark his grave with only a few stones.

Prayer at the Grave

The Torah[8] recounts that Moshe sent twelve spies to probe the Holy Land. When they arrived in Hevron, only Calev went into Me'arat Hamachpelah to prostrate himself on the grave of our

---

8. See *Bamidbar* 13:22 and Rashi, as well as *Sotah* 34b. The commentators and Rashi ask, "How do we know that it was Calev ben Yefuneh who left the explorers to go pray in Hevron?" They answer by the verse (*Bamidbar* 14:24), *I shall bring him to the land where he went*, which is Hevron. For a verse says, *He gave Hevron to Calev* (*Yehoshua* 14).

ancestors. He prayed there that G-d help him not to be swayed by the spies' plot to slander the Holy Land. The Talmud learns this from the verse, *They went up south and he went to Hevron.* Should not the verse say, "and *they* went to Hevron," in the plural? Rava explains that Calev disengaged himself from the explorers' plot and went to pray on the Patriarchs' grave. "My fathers!" he cried. "Pray that I be saved from the explorers' plot!"

The Talmud (*Ta'anit* 16a) presents the rationale behind going to a cemetery on fast days. One reason is to ask the dead to implore Divine mercy on our behalf. The Ran there explains, "It is recommended to pray on the graves of tzaddikim, for prayer at such a place is particularly accepted since there are dead bodies on which Divine blessing rests. Indeed, living tzaddikim are similar to the holy sanctuary and are the abode of the Divine Presence. Not only during their life, but also after their death their burial place is fit to hold Divine abundance. Their bones, which, in their lifetime, were utensils on which rested Divine abundance, still retain their eminence and their honor."

Prayer at the graves of tzaddikim brings about a time of benevolence and mercy On High on behalf of the living.[9] Rabbi Hizkiyah Medini, author of *Sde Hemed*, writes that when the deceased see the living approaching them to recount their sorrows, they take pity on them and are pained by their suffering. Since those pious dead do not merit punishment, G-d has mercy on the living.

These words of our Sages guide the members of our community in every generation. In their high regard for tzaddikim, they are not satisfied with merely visiting their graves; they remain there at length and learn for the elevation of the tzaddik's soul. They recall

---

9. See stories on this topic in *Od Yosef Hai*, pp. 65 and 68.

his merit so that he will pray for them and plead their cases, and those of all the Jewish people—to raise up the Divine Presence from exile and bring about the Final Redemption.

What to Say

A disciple asked the hidden tzaddik Rabbi Yosef Dayan which text to say when praying at graves of tzaddikim. Rabbi Yosef answered, "When you are in front of the tzaddik's grave, say, 'My holy master Rabbi Ploni ben Ploni, may your memory be for a blessing, who rests here. I am your servant. May you find peace. Please, I ask Hakadosh Baruch Hu that by your merit... (State your request)...

"'My holy master Rabbi Ploni ben Ploni, may your memory be for a blessing, who rests here. For all my requests, I learn Torah and give money to charity for the elevation of your soul, *bli neder*. For the unity of the Holy One blessed be He and His *Shechinah*, I learn Torah and give money to charity. May the words of my mouth and the meditations of my heart be pleasing before You, G-d, my Rock and my Redeemer. May the pleasantness of the Almighty, our G-d, be upon us. And to our handiwork, give support for us and thus, our handiwork will endure.'"

A Legacy of Leaders
Vol. I & II

Inspiring Stories and Biographies of Sephardi Hachamim

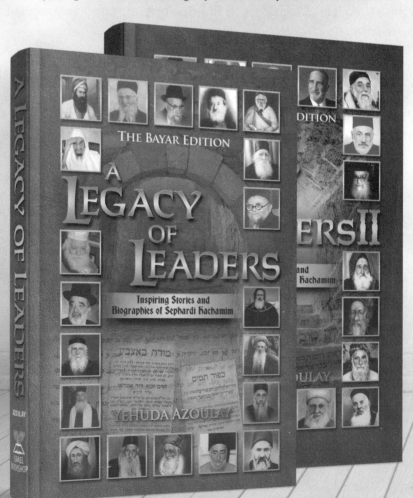